HART

HIGH ADVERSITY
RESILIENCE TRAINING

//////////

CERTIFICATION
MANUAL

Jurie G. Rossouw
Hello Driven

driven
hellodriven.com

High Adversity Resilience Training Certification Manual
Edition 1.0 - 2024

First printed in 2024

ISBN 978-0-9942412-4-5

Crisis Assistance

Hello Driven and HART Instructors do not provide crisis support. If you or someone else requires help, contact your local emergency services:

USA: 911 (General emergency), 988 (Suicide helpline)
UK: 999
Australia: 000
New Zealand: 111

FOREWORD

There are certain occupations that give people a unique experience of life. These include emergency services, healthcare, defense, crisis response, fire and rescue, and others dealing with the more extreme realities of this world.

The voices of many who have experienced not just the work pressures of these occupations, but also the impacts to everyday life and relationships, have contributed and collaborated to create High Adversity Resilience Training – HART.

While HART trains you to sustainably appreciate and perform this meaningful work, it also considers the external part – how can leaders, managers, and supervisors create an environment and culture that supports resilience.

This is where HART takes integrated and connected approach where we all work together to build a culture of resilience. There needs to be a balance of investment in ourselves and an investment in the organization itself to create this culture.

I hope the science-based skills in the HART Certification are valuable to you. Take them with you to support and enhance your life, and where possible, use these lessons to build a world where we can all be stronger together.

All the best in resilience,

Jurie Rossouw
Director, Hello Driven

CONTENTS

INTRODUCTION

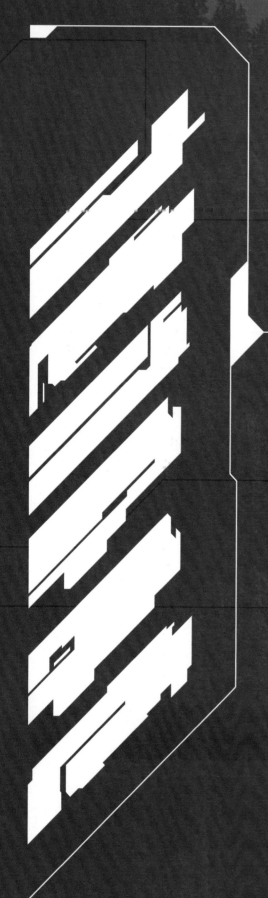

1.1

HART CERTIFICATION OVERVIEW

1.1 HART CERTIFICATION OVERVIEW

High Adversity Resilience Training (HART) consists of a set of advanced life skills designed for those who experience extreme situations in their work. These skills go beyond mental techniques, but also flow through to real world action and building organizations that support resilience at all levels.

The outcome is a culture of resilience. A connecting force that enables those on the front lines to sustainably do the toughest jobs and be effectively prepared for the challenges along the way.

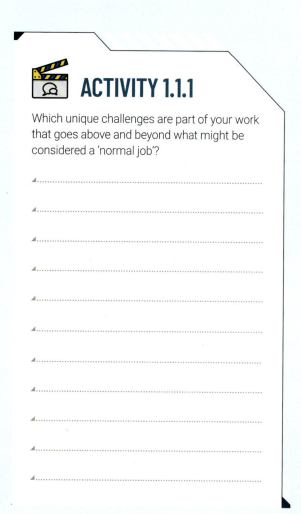

ACTIVITY 1.1.1

Which unique challenges are part of your work that goes above and beyond what might be considered a 'normal job'?

....

....

....

....

....

....

....

....

....

....

1.1.1 What is High Adversity?

HART expands on the latest mental health and resilience research for those in high adversity occupations, providing an advanced approach that recognizes the unique challenges faced in these roles. Most resilience programs train people to deal with the everyday stress of life. These skills are important for everyone to learn and make the most out of life.

However, those in high adversity occupations deal regularly with the harsh realities of life - situations that others may only deal with once in a lifetime. This is why the **HART Certification** was developed to include advanced and specialized skills needed for these occupations.

Across the range of high adversity occupations, there are challenges such as:

- **Life or death** situations
- Managing **crises** and **high-risk** situations
- Working with **inevitability** - palliative care, degenerative diseases, disability
- Work long **shifts** and/or at unusual times
- Helping **distraught people**, often on the worst day of their lives
- Witnessing and treating **traumatic injuries** and handling remains (human or animal)
- Being at risk of **physical threats and harm**

Most of these are challenges that the general population rarely faces, but for you, it might be a normal day.

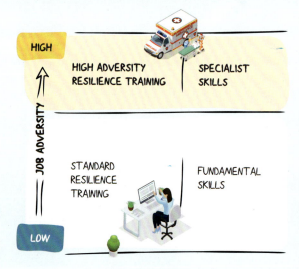

1.1.2   HART Occupations

There are various occupations that fall under the 'high adversity' banner. These include:

- Emergency medicine (Paramedic, EMT, ambulance based)
- Healthcare (hospital, clinics, aged care)
- Fire, rescue, emergency services
- Law enforcement, security services
- Emergency dispatch, crisis call centers
- Military, defense, and armed forces
- Certain professionals, such as law, investigation, therapy, education, and carers

The skills developed through this training is helpful not only for those performing the work themselves, but also for family members and those in leadership who create the environment within which high adversity workers operate.

As we will learn later on, creating a supportive environment at home and work is crucial to be able to sustain the ability to perform and enjoy this type of work.

1.1.3   Why Training Is Needed

Because of the unique challenges faced in high adversity roles, there are specific risks to be mindful of[1]:

- Higher rates of **mental illness** than other occupations (anxiety, depression, PTSI)
- Higher rates of **suicide** than other occupations
- Higher risk of **compassion fatigue and burnout**
- Issues with sleep, challenges with shift work
- **Social disconnection**, isolation, and loneliness

These risks are very real, and it's helpful to create open dialogue about these. Particularly since these can be prevented through targeted training, exactly in the same way that proper equipment training helps to avoid injuries.

HART has been developed to address these risks proactively. By completing this training, you can prepare yourself for the challenges of your work and reduce these risks, helping you to appreciate the work you do in the long run.

1   Ponder, W. N., Walters, K., Simons, J. S., Simons, R. M., Jetelina, K. K., & Carbajal, J. (2023). Network analysis of distress, suicidality, and resilience in a treatment seeking sample of first responders. *Journal of affective disorders*, 320, 742-750.

1.1.4 HART's Origin

HART builds on the peer-reviewed **Predictive 6 Factor Resilience Model**[2] **(PR6)**, providing a comprehensive mind-body understanding of resilience that enables both assessment and development of strength-based resilience skills.

This model includes a neuroscience-based approach to build prevention into the wiring of the brain, giving us a natural ability to be resilient in more situations as we continuously practice and embed these skills.

These combine with validated advanced resilience strategies that were tailored with input from high adversity community members, spanning emergency medicine, law enforcement, emergency services, and defense.

The resulting HART program is an advanced and science-based resilience course specifically designed for the challenges you might face, focusing on **what you can do proactively** to mitigate the risks related to this work.

This course is also useful for family and friends of those in a high adversity occupation. This will help to learn the same techniques and better understand the challenges of the work, as well as the techniques to help maintain resilience.

The HART Certification is part of the overall **HART Approach**, which covers a comprehensive program to build a culture of resilience, stretching from the leaders through to family members at home.

1.1.5 HART Certification Program

HART includes a **specialized training regime** to build resilience capacity for high adversity occupational challenges.

This includes fourteen modules across the six domains of resilience. Within each domain you will learn skills specifically targeted towards building proactive strength and capacity that enhances resilience over time.

The modules covered through the HART Certification course and in this manual are listed below:

HART Introduction
1. Fundamentals & Neuroscience

VISION
2. Connecting Purpose

HEALTH
3. Managing Work Hours

REASONING
4. Sustainable Compartmenting
5. Optimizing Thoughts & Behaviors
6. Concrete vs Abstract Processing

COMPOSURE
7. Brain-Balanced Breathing
8. High Adversity Reappraisal

TENACITY
9. Mental Load Management
10. Three Good Things

COLLABORATION
11. High Quality Connections
12. Grief & Growth
13. Strong Relationships
14. High Adversity Humor

Each module provides practical knowledge and skills that increase resilience and prepares you for different aspects of your work. Mastering these takes time and effort, though the **reward is in being able to effectively manage the challenges along the way and get the most out of life.**

---

2   Rossouw, J.G., Rossouw, P.J., Paynter, C., Ward, A., Khnana, P. (2017). Predictive 6 Factor Resilience Scale – Domains of Resilience and Their Role as Enablers of Job Satisfaction. *International Journal of Neuropsychotherapy*, 2(1), 25-40.

INTRODUCTION

1.2

RESILIENCE CULTURE

1.2 RESILIENCE CULTURE

The concept and definition of resilience has evolved significantly over time. Going from simplistic definitions such as 'bouncing back', through to more advanced holistic understandings such as the six domains in the PR6 model, alongside modernizing the definition to **'Advancing despite adversity'**.

RESILIENCE IS NOT ALL ABOUT CHANGING **HOW YOU THINK**

The key shift in focus is away from simply 'bouncing back', which implies returning to the status quo. Instead, we shift towards 'advancing', meaning continual growth and the sustainable pursuit of your purpose.

We now expand our definition of resilience to not be purely about the individual, but also their surrounding environment, which includes the people we connect with. This creates the concept of **Connected Resilience** – the resilience that arises from our support networks combined with our own personal resilience capacity.

This means that resilience is not just about yourself, but also about how we connect and support each other.

Importantly, resilience is not all about changing how you think.

While much of building resilience revolves around changing how you interpret and react to events, it's also vital to consider additional factors. These factors can either contribute to or hinder the development of resilience.

This means that, at times, resilience may necessitate changes and improvements in the environment itself. Understanding this means gaining knowledge about the prevalent challenges and recognizing the need to cultivate both personal resilience and a resilient culture within the work environment.

Three Areas of Challenge

Overall, there are three main categories of challenges people face in high adversity work[3] :

- **Operational** challenges
- **Organizational** challenges
- **Relational** challenges, meaning relationships with family and friends, etc

While there are other types of challenges, these are the most significant contributors to the risks that form part of high adversity work.

1.2.1 Operational

The most common challenges that come to mind when considering these occupations are what is classed as 'Operational'. These include:

- Manage **crises** and being under **extreme pressure** to perform in the moment
- Exposure to **trauma and death**, which can include witnessing, preventing, handling, treating major injuries, or for some also inflicting (defense, police)
- Higher **personal risk** of injury and death
- Difficult interactions with the **public**, such as delivering bad news, dealing with combative people, and so on

These aspects are often what attracts people to these lines of work – a sense of calling to make a difference, to help, to protect people, regions, or their country, or performing tasks that may be too difficult for others to do.

---

3   Hamling, K. (2018). *Wellbeing across occupations and in the emergency services: A mixed methods study* (Doctoral dissertation, Auckland University of Technology).

1.2.2 Organizational

Beyond Operational challenges, we find that the work often involves less visible factors that may seem minor initially, though over time these add up if not managed effectively.

These are classed as 'Organizational' challenges, or sometimes called 'administrative' challenges. These include:

- **Shift work**, fly-in-fly-out schedules, deployments, often leading to irregular sleeping patterns
- Large amounts of documentation, **paperwork**, and administrative duties
- Adhering to rigid **procedures**, requiring extensive study and potential harsh consequences when procedures are not strictly followed
- Demanding or difficult **training regimes**
- Not having all the **resources** or tools needed to do the work, lack of necessary tools, or complex procedures to request resources
- **Stigma**, such as people always expecting you to be strong, being expected to simply deal with traumatic exposures or the challenges of the work
- Fitting into rigid **command structures**
- Extreme **time pressures** to complete administrative tasks
- **Conflict** or issues with staff or managers, including feelings of unfairness when it comes to promotions, shifts, duties, and so on
- Conflicting agendas, **unclear priorities**

Isolated instances of organizational challenges are manageable, however many challenges here over time can wear down our ability to be resilient and create vulnerability when dealing with operational challenges.

Research found that people who are under high organizational load to be a higher risk of developing Post Traumatic Stress Injury (PTSI)[3]. This highlights how resilience is not simply about our own individual capacity, but also about how leaders, support staff, and family members can help to create a better environment that supports resilience.

Creating a better environment increases your ability to manage extreme operational challenges over time.

EXAMPLE

Breaking Concrete

An analogy is what often happens with concrete. The purpose of concrete is to hold up and support heavy structures, and it excels at this function, often able to do this for hundreds of years.

However, small amounts of water can filter through the pores of the concrete and make it through to the steel reinforcement bars inside. The water causes rust to form inside the concrete structure, resulting in pressure from the inside.

Concrete is very capable of withstanding pressure from the outside, but internal pressure causes cracks, resulting in pieces breaking and falling off. This is called concrete degradation, which causes the overall structure to weaken.

This is how a little bit of water can make something as strong as concrete fail at the job it is so good at.

Still, these challenges can be prevented by managing the environment the concrete is in, allowing it to perform effectively throughout its lifespan.

This is the same for organizational challenges – these seemingly small environmental aspects of the work can add up and erode our ability to do the work we are good at.

1.2.3 Relational

The third aspect of challenges that often form part of this work is classed as 'Relational', meaning the challenges relating to maintaining relationships. These include:

- ◢ Work stress can lead people to **disengage from partners and children**
- ◢ **Not wanting to share** what happened during the day to save family members from being distressed, resulting in a sense of isolation
- ◢ Confidential nature of work may also **prevent what can be shared** with family members
- ◢ Long shifts and work hours can **leave little time with family members and friends**

- ◢ The work can make it difficult to **build and maintain relationships** with family and even friends
- ◢ **Difficulty in relating** to civilians, who may often not understand the reality of the work, leading to fewer opportunities to form broader friendship groups and find partners

These challenges are common with high adversity work and require ongoing effort to manage over time.

The skills within the HART Certification course are designed to help on a personal level to **proactively manage these aspects** so they become less of a challenge, and more something that you are actively taking care of.

1.2.4   HART Culture

Managing these different types of challenges is a task for the whole community. Working together is what enables those facing the main operational challenges to be able to sustainably perform the work and avoid the risks that may arise over time. This is where we consider the cultural aspect of resilience.

SUPPORTING EACH OTHER TO **ADVANCE DESPITE ADVERSITY**

Specifically, we're interested in **how we can create a culture that enables resilience, rather than requires it.** This is an important distinction, since historically people in high adversity occupations have simply been expected to put up with the challenges of the job, shrug it off and move on. However, we now understand that resilience is not simply about the individual, but rather a combination of the individual with the environment and connection we have with people around us.

ACTIVITY 1.2.1

Considering these different types of challenges, which have you found to affect you?

Operational:

....

....

....

....

....

....

Organizational:

....

....

....

....

....

....

Relational:

....

....

....

....

....

....

Defining HART Culture

Through this concept of connection, we can define the concept of HART Culture as follows:

Supporting each other to advance despite adversity.

The HART program overall embodies this approach by expanding resilience elements and training at all levels, since all members of the broader community have roles to play, including:

- **Leaders** who have an overarching responsibility to support a culture of resilience and endorse programs that continually evolves the organizational environment
- **Management** who directly influence organizational challenges, balancing broader goals with individual needs, and maintains culture at a team level

- **Participants** as the front-line operators performing the work, joining in with programs to learn and adopt skills that support mental health personally and in colleagues
- **Family** and friends who play a role in understanding the challenges, understanding the skills the enable sustainability, and providing a supportive and open environment

At an organizational level, these factors can be **assessed and measured** to better understand over time what the needs are and where effort can best be focused.

To establish consistency among these community stakeholders, it is important to establish principles that set the tone for how we interact with each other and define what environment we create.

As an example, here are four principles that can define HART Culture:

- **Support** - We are always there for each other, and we talk about the things that are difficult
- **Open** - We understand our work is tough and we are open about it
- **Learn** - We invest in constantly learning about how to handle the challenges we face
- **Advance** - We are constantly growing and advancing towards our goals - always becoming better together

Resilience culture therefore means that individually we are strong, but **together we are stronger.**

ACTIVITY 1.2.2

Considering these four principles of HART Culture:

Which principles are we doing well?

....

....

....

....

....

....

Which can we improve?

....

....

....

....

....

....

1.2.5 HART Approach

The overall HART Approach combines a comprehensive plan that includes all members of the community who each have their role to play, then through different integrated training programs, each learn to work towards creating a culture of resilience.

The phases are as follows:

1 **Identify Stakeholders** that are involved in the community that makes up the organization. These are the key initial groups to work with and progress on to the continuous program phase

2 **Design Sustainability** refers to building a program that will not simply be a one-off exercise, but rather an ongoing comprehensive effort to build a culture of resilience that lasts. This may include incorporating HART into other existing programs

3 **Implement HART** into the organization, including all program elements that are part of the design, including embedding program champions, running HART Certification courses, performing assessment, giving access to digital tools, as well as making training available to family members to implement training at home

4 **Evaluate & Improve** the program, meaning measure the cultural impact so that lessons learned can be incorporated into the design through the **Improvement Loop**, enabling people to work together to continuously improve the environment and be stronger together.

HART Program Approach

1. IDENTIFY STAKEHOLDERS

Leaders
Executive layer - key leaders and decision-makers required for top-level endorsement

Managers
All management and supervisory roles, through to managers of ground-level staff

Staff
Operational front-line workers, members, volunteers, and support staff

2. DESIGN SUSTAINABILITY

Culture Design
Clarify cultural goals to embed resilience as a key value of the organisation. Agree on program elements needed to achieve cultural uplift and sustainability

Management Training
Educate management on risk factors and own responsibility to lead by example. Put meaningful effort into improving organisational risk factors

Coordinated Launch
Communicate to all staff through leaders and managers the program to be launched through coordinated campaign for high awareness

3. IMPLEMENT HART

Embed Champions
Ground-level and management staff to champion resilience

Workshops & Trainers
Certified HART trainers to run workshops and live training

Assessments
PR6 assessment to track starting point and change over time

Digital Access (app)
Virtual delivery of HART program to scale ongoing reinforcement

Family Access
App and training webinars for family of staff to extend impact

4. EVALUATE & IMPROVE

Measure & Report
Ongoing assessment of progress across risk factors:
• Operational
• Organisational
• Relational

PR6 assessment to measure changes in resilience domains:
• Vision
• Composure,
• Reasoning
• Tenacity
• Collaboration
• Health

Track program impact and identify opportunities for improvement.

Improvement Loop Continually learn, enhance integration of program implementation. On-board new staff.

INTRODUCTION

1.3

NEUROSCIENCE OF HIGH ADVERSITY

1.3 NEUROSCIENCE OF HIGH ADVERSITY

Your brain is the most complex machine you'll ever own. This concept is important, since when there are machines you need to operate at work, you receive training to use them effectively and safely.

This training is necessary so you can properly do your work, be it to help people, protect people, or otherwise. **Good training saves lives.**

Yet, very few people receive training in how to operate the most complex machine of all – the brain – a biological machine that helps you operate all the other machines, tools, relationships and everything else in your life.

ACTIVITY 1.3.1

Have you noticed some of these high stress effects, in yourself or others?

....

....

....

....

....

....

....

....

....

....

....

....

....

....

1.3.1 The Brain on High Adversity

The concept of high adversity work is that these are occupations that face stress and challenge beyond what can be expected in 'normal' job (like general office work, retail, and so on). That is not to say that other jobs don't have challenges or face stress, but the kind of exposure is different.

For a 'normal' person, one major emergency can bring on PTSI that might take years to resolve. However, these are situations often faced daily by those on the front lines. Yet you need to:

◢ **Be calm and in control** during emergencies when other people are panicking

◢ Deal with the **cumulative impact** of managing emergencies and tough situations on a regular basis

These aspects are often what attracts people to these lines of work – a sense of calling to make a difference, to help, to protect people, regions, or their country, or performing tasks that may be too difficult for others to do.

The Brain Under Stress

What does it look like when this kind of 'damage' happens in the brain? Here we notice:

◢ **Sleep Disorders –** Chronic exposure to high-stress environments can disrupt normal sleep patterns, causing issues like insomnia which can deteriorate overall health

◢ **Burnout –** This refers to a state of chronic physical and emotional exhaustion, a depletion of your energy and resources which stifles both productivity and creativity

◢ **Depression and Anxiety –** High adversity can lead to mood disorders like depression and anxiety, characterized by persistent feelings of sadness, hopelessness, and heightened fears and worries

◢ **Post Traumatic Stress Injury (PTSI) –** This is a complex condition where individuals struggle to move past the traumatic events they have witnessed or experienced

◢ **Secondary Trauma –** Often professionals develop symptoms like PTSI simply by helping or wanting to help a traumatized or suffering person

◢ **Compassion Fatigue –** This refers to the gradual lessening of compassion over time, often as a protective mechanism against the overwhelming emotions associated with caring for those in distress

- **Suicidal Ideation –** In extreme cases, the unrelenting pressure and the amassed psychological distress can foster thoughts of suicide, an important time to reach out for help

In high-stress professions, it's not enough to just be mentally strong or resilient. Believing that one should just "deal with it" can lead to serious problems. It's important to understand that being good at your job doesn't automatically protect your brain from the stress involved.

That's why it's crucial to take active steps to strengthen your resilience through preventative training, especially in jobs with high adversity, where these problems are more common than in other types of jobs.

Brain Benefits of Resilience Training

Investing time and effort to resilience training have many advantages that not only enhance your work performance but can significantly improve your personal life as well. Here, we delve deeper into the various benefits that such training can give you, fostering a meaningful and fulfilling career journey.

- **Being More Prepared –** One of the primary benefits of this training is cultivating a state of readiness to tackle any challenges that come your way. Being prepared means possessing the skills and mindset necessary to anticipate potential hurdles and formulate strategies to overcome them with confidence

- **Mitigating Mental Load –** Resilience training plays a pivotal role in cushioning the mental impacts inherent in demanding work environments. By equipping you with coping mechanisms and stress management techniques, it fosters a mentally healthy workspace, reducing the toll it takes on your mind

- **Increased Job Satisfaction –** Embracing these lessons can help you derive greater joy and satisfaction from your work. This, in turn, leads to an enriched work experience where you not only perform tasks efficiently but also find enjoyment and fulfillment in your professional pursuits, including the less glamorous parts

- **Calm and Effective Crisis Management –** In moments of crisis, a calm demeanor paired with effective problem-solving skills make a significant difference. Resilience training helps in nurturing these qualities, enabling you to navigate extreme situations with clarity and decisiveness, thereby emerging as a reliable source of support and leadership

- **Enhanced Analytical Thinking –** This training fosters an environment where you can develop more accurate and analytical thinking. It be applied to make informed and sound decisions

- **Career Growth and Development –** As you adapt and grow through resilience training, you may notice advancements in your career trajectory. The skills acquired not only make you an asset to your organization but also pave the way for personal growth and career development, leading to a series of progressive milestones in your professional journey

- **Developing Mental Discipline –** Training gives you the skills to see challenges not as obstacles, but as opportunities for growth. At the same time, it increases your mental discipline to take on difficult tasks and routines, stick to training and maintain relationships in the long term

- **Better Communication Skills –** The training also facilitates the development of robust communication skills, empowering you to build meaningful connections with many different types of people. These skills are vital in fostering a collaborative work environment and can also translate to more fulfilling personal relationships

- **Building Stronger Relationships –** As a result of improved communication and understanding, you're more likely to foster better relationships, both professionally and personally. The training equips you to understand and relate to others more effectively, thereby building stronger and more meaningful connections with those you value

Understanding and embracing these benefits can serve as a protective shield, safeguarding you throughout a long and successful career. Engaging in resilience training is not just an investment in your professional growth but a commitment to nurturing a life enriched with understanding, satisfaction, and mutual respect.

NOTES

_____
_____
_____
_____
_____
_____
_____
_____
_____
_____
_____
_____
_____
_____
_____
_____

After all, this training is not about you becoming a neuroscientist, but rather to **learn practical skills you can use to improve your life.**

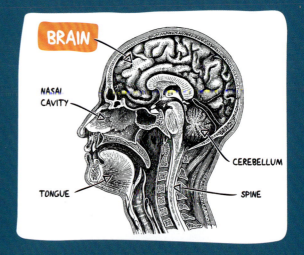

While complex in many ways, we are interested in two key areas:

▴ The Limbic Brain, or LB

▴ And the Prefrontal Cortex, or PFC

By simplifying it like this, it makes it much easier to use the concepts in the heat of the moment, and to understand the general idea of this resilience training.

1.3.2 Simplifying the Brain

The brain is complicated. Even after decades of studying with modern science, we still don't fully understand how the brain works, though we have learned a lot – enough to be able to learn some important insights that help you master the biological machine in your head.

With the brain being as complicated as it is, it helps to simplify and understand it in a practical sense. For this training, we will oversimplify the brain, though we do this purposefully to make it easier to use resilience skills in the moment of stress and emergency.

1.3.3 The Limbic Brain

This is the oldest part of the brain and is primarily focused on survival. This part of the brain evolved over 100 million years ago. That means its power in the brain is very strong and deeply wired.

▴ Its role is to help detect threats and quickly respond to help us survive

▴ To respond quickly, it doesn't want you to think deeply about things, so it reduces your critical thinking ability by reducing blood flow to the PFC

▴ What this means is that you might not take the best action, since you're not thinking all too clearly at that moment

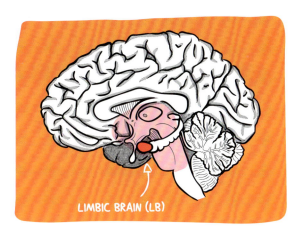

LIMBIC BRAIN (LB)

When Does the Limbic Brain Activate?

When the LB activates, it results in sudden emotional reactions. It does this through what is usually called the fight, flight, or freeze response. Here are different examples of when the LB might activate more strongly:

- **Perceiving a Threat –** When you sense danger or a potential threat, the limbic brain activates to prepare your body to protect itself and survive

- Experiencing Emotional Moments – During intense emotional experiences, such as joy, fear, sadness, or excitement, the limbic brain is at work to process these emotions

- **Social Interactions –** Engaging in social interactions, including forming bonds, empathizing with others, or experiencing social exclusion, can activate the limbic brain

- **Learning and Memory Formation –** The limbic brain plays a crucial role in memory consolidation, helping in the formation and retrieval of memories, particularly those related to emotions (this plays a key role in PTSI)

- **Sensory Processing –** Upon receiving sensory information, like smells or sounds, that are associated with past experiences or emotions, the limbic brain might activate

- **Regulating Appetite and Food Intake –** It is also involved in the regulation of appetite, becoming active during the perception of food cues and the enjoyment of food

- **Engaging in Reward-seeking Behaviors –** When you engage in activities perceived as rewarding or pleasurable, including enjoying music or indulging in hobbies, the limbic brain gets activated

- **Drug Use and Addiction –** The limbic brain is significantly involved in the processes of drug addiction, where it mediates the effects of drugs on reward pathways and emotional responses

- **Lack of Sleep –** Missing out on quality sleep increases the reactivity of the limbic brain, making emotional responses to different situations more likely

As you can see, some events that activate the LB are positive, though there are times when the LB activates when it is not helpful. Recognizing when the limbic brain might be active can help in understanding emotional and behavioral responses in different situations, offering insights into the complex workings of the human brain.

The key challenge is that **modern problems are too complex for the LB to solve**. This means it is useful for us to control how strongly the LB activates in certain circumstances, so that we can stay calm and in control when we need to be.

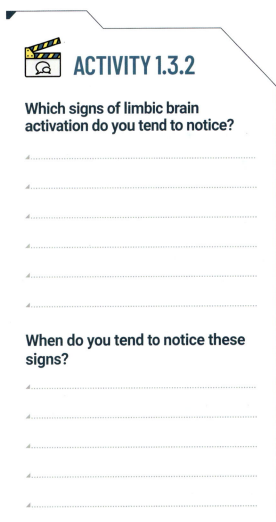

ACTIVITY 1.3.2

Which signs of limbic brain activation do you tend to notice?

....

....

....

....

....

....

When do you tend to notice these signs?

....

....

....

....

....

....

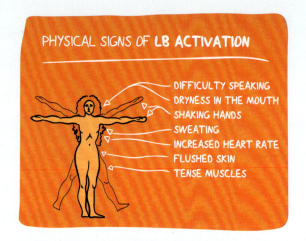

PHYSICAL SIGNS OF **LB ACTIVATION**

- DIFFICULTY SPEAKING
- DRYNESS IN THE MOUTH
- SHAKING HANDS
- SWEATING
- INCREASED HEART RATE
- FLUSHED SKIN
- TENSE MUSCLES

Signs of Limbic Brain Activation

How do you know when the LB is activating? There are clear signs we can notice, such as:

- **Difficulty Speaking –** Reduced blood flow to the frontal cortex makes it harder to think and speak, leading to communication challenges
- **Dryness in the Mouth –** Including difficulty to swallow
- **Increased Heart Rate –** As part of the fight-or-flight response, the heart pumps blood faster to make more resources available to the body
- **Heightened Emotional Responses –** Often appearing as intense emotions such as anger, fear, sadness, grief, pain, but also happiness and excitement
- **Sweating –** Fluctuations in body temperature, including sweating is a common sign
- **Fluctuations in Breathing Rate –** Breathing may increase or become more pronounced, preparing the body to respond to perceived challenges
- **Skin and Muscle Changes –** Including muscles becoming tense as they prepare fight or flee, as well as skin becoming pale on the body as blood is pulled to the muscles, while the face might be flushed or pale
- **Facial Expressions –** Often creating involuntary facial expressions, from disgust, to anger, to smiling
- **Memory Flashbacks –** You might experience flashbacks or vivid memory recalls, especially of emotionally charged events, as the limbic brain plays a role in memory consolidation and retrieval

- **Digestive Responses –** You may experience stomach butterflies or other gastrointestinal responses, as the limbic brain influences the autonomic nervous system, which can affect the digestive system
- **Pupil Dilation –** Your pupils may dilate as a response to emotional or environmental stimuli mediated by the limbic brain
- **Altered Sleep Patterns –** Changes in sleep patterns might occur, as the limbic brain is involved in regulating various stages of the sleep cycle
- **Enhanced Sensory Perception –** Sensory perceptions, like smells or sounds, might become more vivid, as the limbic brain is involved in processing sensory information, particularly when linked to emotional experiences
- **Cravings and Urges –** Experiencing cravings or urges, particularly related to food or substances, as the limbic brain is involved in reward pathways and appetite regulation

Levels of Limbic Brain Activation

Activation of the LB is more than simply on or off. In a simplified way, the relative strength of LB activation is important since higher activation has serious effects on your mental state. This chart illustrates this concept

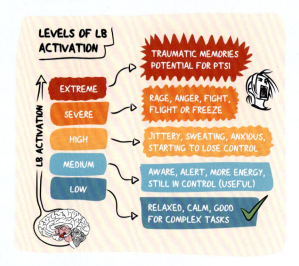

LEVELS OF LB ACTIVATION

LB ACTIVATION

- EXTREME → TRAUMATIC MEMORIES POTENTIAL FOR PTSI
- SEVERE → RAGE, ANGER, FIGHT, FLIGHT OR FREEZE
- HIGH → JITTERY, SWEATING, ANXIOUS, STARTING TO LOSE CONTROL
- MEDIUM
- LOW → AWARE, ALERT, MORE ENERGY, STILL IN CONTROL (USEFUL)
- RELAXED, CALM, GOOD FOR COMPLEX TASKS ✓

From this diagram we can see:

- A **low level of LB activation** is when you feel relaxed and calm – a level that's good for working on complex tasks
- Going up to a **medium level of activation** can be useful in some situations when you need more energy and to be more alert, putting the adrenaline to good use
- At a high level of activation, you start to lose control a bit, as you feel more anxious, sweating, hands may start to shake, etc.
- A **severe level of activation** tends to bring on unhelpful responses, like flying into a rage, freezing due to fear, or feeling an urge to get away
- At the top end, an **extreme level of activation** is when a single event can be so traumatic that PTSI and other disorders may form. This is because extreme LB activation creates powerful emotionally charged memories that may require therapy and significant effort to overcome

Note – this is a simplified view for practical purposes. The actual processes are complex and intricate. LB activation can spike from Medium to Extreme in less than a second, making preventative training very important.

The key point - Being able to control your brain means that you can manage these levels of activations to suit the situation.

This example shows what activation may look like in someone with a highly reactive limbic brain (a brain that has not been trained in resilience skills).

Looking at the scale, we see high to extreme levels of activation for the different types of events that are mapped out on this chart.

Hearing a loud noise, or public speaking is often scary. Perhaps the prospect of a long-term relationship even? Being wrong about something? For some, these are events that strongly activate the LB and result in responses that are severe and may seem out of character for the person.

The problem in these situations is that the person is likely to react emotionally and impulsively, resulting in actions that are not helpful to improve the situation or perform properly. This may result in feelings of failure, guilt, or shame, resulting in a vicious circle of further LB activation.

To temper these responses and create useful responses that improve the situation, we need to get to know the Prefrontal Cortex.

ACTIVITY 1.3.3

Thinking about the example of The Untrained Brain, what might it be like to be this person?

....
....
....
....
....
....
....
....
....
....
....
....
....

THE **UNTRAINED BRAIN**

LB ACTIVATION IS TOO HIGH OVERALL.

EXTREME
SEVERE
HIGH
MEDIUM
LOW

LB DEFAULT THREAT RESPONSE

LOUD NOISE
PUBLIC SPEAKING
OBJECT FLYING AT YOU
TALKING TO NEW PEOPLE
BEING WRONG ABOUT SOMETHING
LONG TERM RELATIONSHIPS
BEING APPROACHED FROM BEHIND
DOGS
ADDRESSED BY SUPERIOR

1.3.4 Prefrontal Cortex

This is the newest part of the brain, having only evolved over the last few hundred thousand years. In terms of evolution, that's very recent.

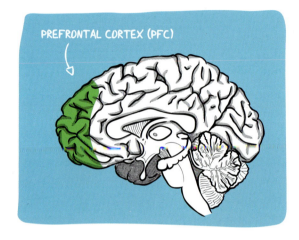

PREFRONTAL CORTEX (PFC)

In comparison to other animals, the size of the PFC sets humans apart. It's this part of the brain that's given humans the ability to:

- ◢ Develop language
- ◢ Thinking complex thoughts
- ◢ Develop ideas
- ◢ Invent tools
- ◢ Creatively solve problems
- ◢ Be resourceful
- ◢ Plan ahead
- ◢ Learn complex skills
- ◢ And create the highly technologically advanced society we live in today

It's also the part of your brain that is **most important in your work**, having to quickly solve complex problems using your vast knowledge and training to work through emergencies and even life-saving challenges.

Given the complex problems you face in modern times, and especially when doing your work, you need your PFC to function at its best. Therefore, the ability of the LB to inhibit the PFC is not so helpful. How can we then manage this activation more effectively? The answer lies in how the brain is connected, and how we can change these connections.

1.3.5 Neural Connections

The brain is full of connections. There are over 80 billion neurons in the brain, and a single neuron can have 70,000 connections. **These connections encode your personality, knowledge, beliefs, thoughts, and actions.**

At birth, the **brain is 'preconfigured'** with certain connections to give it a starting point. From there, the brain quickly adapts connections through early childhood experiences as the brain learns about the world.

Because the brain mainly adapted to survive physical threats like wild animals hunting us in ancient times, the brain isn't by default prepared to deal with the modern complex challenges we face. And the brain especially isn't prepared to do high adversity work.

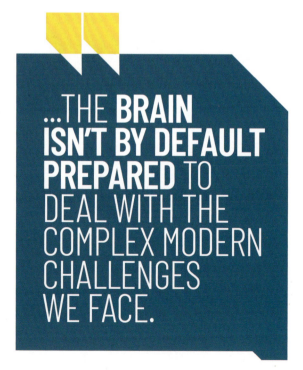

...THE **BRAIN ISN'T BY DEFAULT PREPARED** TO DEAL WITH THE COMPLEX MODERN CHALLENGES WE FACE.

By default, the brain prefers to get enraged and fight, or run away. You can imagine how this default response from the brain wouldn't be helpful during an emergency, or maybe when you need to resolve something with a loved one.

What's important about this is that by the time you are an adult, **the brain still holds many of the old connections that can lead to unhelpful thoughts and behaviors.**

These old unhelpful connections need to be challenged and optimized, ideally through proactive training.

Optimizing Connections

An important quality of the brain is that it can be changed. This is called **neuroplasticity**.

Plasticity means that you can **break old habits** and unhelpful ways of thinking, and instead **build new and better habits**. How does this work practically? Simple:

- You learn new skills and techniques
- And then you practice them

As you learn and practice, you create new neural connections in your brain that cement this skill in your mind. The more you practice, the more natural it becomes, because the neural connections become stronger the more you use them.

Repetition builds neural connections. This is exactly the same for building your resilience and mental toughness. That also means you can't just read about resilience skills once. **You need to practice it and live it for your brain to become stronger.** As you practice resilience skills the neural connections that enable them becomes stronger, and your ability to be resilient becomes easier and more natural.

The Relationship Between the PFC and the LB

The PFC and LB have a close connection. If the LB detects some type of danger, it can reduce blood flow and functioning of the PFC. That means when you panic, feel fear, or feel anxious, the LB makes it harder for you to solve problems and think on your feet.

However, tough situations are exactly when you need to be at your best.

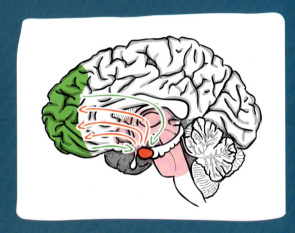

By default, the LB has a lot of control over the PFC, meaning it can easily **reduce your ability to think clearly**. Frequent and strong activation of the LB can result in other effects too. It can:

- **Create powerful fear-based memories** from traumatic experiences, leading to risk of PTSI
- **Accumulate stressful experiences** that result in burnout and feeling overwhelmed
- **Cause over-awareness of danger**, even in non-dangerous situations, leading to anxiety disorders

What resilience training really does is **teach you skills to control LB activation and make it work for you.**

1.3.6 Training the Brain

Thinking back to The Untrained Brain before where we saw someone having a very reactive limbic brain, we can now consider what it might be like for this person to change their brain. We can imagine the person doing resilience training, changing beliefs, practicing certain behaviors, and in doing so causing the wiring of the brain to change.

ACTIVITY 1.3.4

Where have you noticed changes in these types of neural connections to help you be calmer in some situations?

⊿...

⊿...

⊿...

⊿...

⊿...

⊿...

⊿...

⊿...

⊿...

⊿...

⊿...

⊿...

⊿...

⊿...

As the brain's wiring changes, we find that the emotions that arise from the brain change, and it becomes easier to stay calm and in control in different situations. For example, let's say our test subject practices some new skills, such as:

⊿ Learn how to approach dogs and not fear them unless they show signs of aggression

⊿ Understand that it's ok to be wrong about something, and embrace the opportunity to learn new things

⊿ Learn how to quickly assess new people and be open to them

⊿ Build skills with public speaking to feel capable to do it

Here we have a picture of how LB reactivity reduces in a resilient brain, where the connections in the brain have been trained through resilience training to respond more constructively to different events.

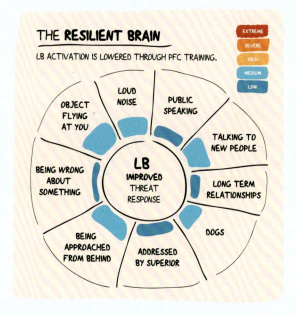

Much of what you'll learn in the HART Certification course is about two aspects:

⊿ Teaching you various techniques to **manage the activation of your limbic brain**

⊿ Developing skills to **maximize activation of your prefrontal cortex**

NOTES

....
....
....
....
....
....
....
....
....
....
....
....
....
....
....
....
....
....
....
....
....
....
....
....
....
....
....
....

SCAN ME

High Adversity Neuroscience
in the **Driven Resilience App**

Scan the code below to access the skill in the app. Make sure you are **logged into the app** for the code to work.

app.hellodriven.com/activities/1229

INTRODUCTION

1.4

SIX DOMAINS OF RESILIENCE

1.4 SIX DOMAINS OF RESILIENCE

While we can define resilience as advancing despite adversity, achieving this as an ongoing outcome is not a result of just one behavior or process. Instead, resilience consists of **groups of behaviors, skills, and beliefs.** These groups are called **domains**.

Understanding these domains allows us to measure resilience for an individual to identify the starting point, highlight areas for focus, and track improvement over time. The better we understand these domains, the more targeted action we can take to build our resilience and create a culture of resilience.

The measurement tool we developed at Driven is called the **Predictive 6-Factor Resilience Scale**[2], or **PR6** for short, and identified the following domains of resilience:

- **Vision**, which is about goal setting and a sense of purpose
- **Composure**, which is about regulating emotions and managing stress
- **Reasoning**, which is about problem-solving and readiness for change
- **Tenacity**, which is about perseverance and bouncing back
- **Collaboration**, which is about support networks and connecting with others
- **Health**, which is about adequate sleep, nutrition, and exercise

Domains interact with each other and function together to meet the basic needs of the brain. A weakness in one domain can affect others, and conversely, improving one can improve other domains.

The PR6 consolidates decades of prior research and integrates the domains of resilience into their neurobiological foundations.

1.4.1 Vision

Clarity of purpose, meaning, and goals is arguably the most important component of resilience. After all, we can only advance if we have something to advance towards, which in this case is a purpose, a sense of meaning and goals. This includes: our commitment to pursue our goals, maintaining a hopeful outlook, as well as the vision we have of what we aspire to become. Together, these are summarized as the domain of Vision. Within Vision, we will explore a skill called **Connected Purpose**.

1.4.2 Composure

Regulating emotions and managing stress constructively is what the Composure domain is about. Through our home and work life we will invariably face stressful times and our emotions will fluctuate – that is completely natural. What is important, however, is how we deal with it when it happens.

Emotions are produced by the limbic brain, based on what we experience and how we instinctively think about the situation. However, as we know now, we can modify this default behavior through directed use of the PFC. By resetting our expectations and actively identifying when we have an emotional reaction, we can stay calm and in control when facing difficult situations. Composure, therefore, considers our ability to maintain a state of mental equilibrium so that we can function effectively when we need it most.

In the Composure domain, we'll explore the skills of **Brain Balanced Breathing**, as well as **High Adversity Reappraisal**.

1.4.3 Reasoning

Creative problem-solving, anticipating and planning for scenarios, readiness for change, resourcefulness and innovation are all part of the Reasoning domain.

The major role of Reasoning in resilience is to help us use our whole brain to think our way through difficult situations. A high Reasoning ability means we do not resort to destructive emotional tactics that the limbic brain prefers. Instead, we take long-term goals into account and make unusual connections to reach a constructive outcome.

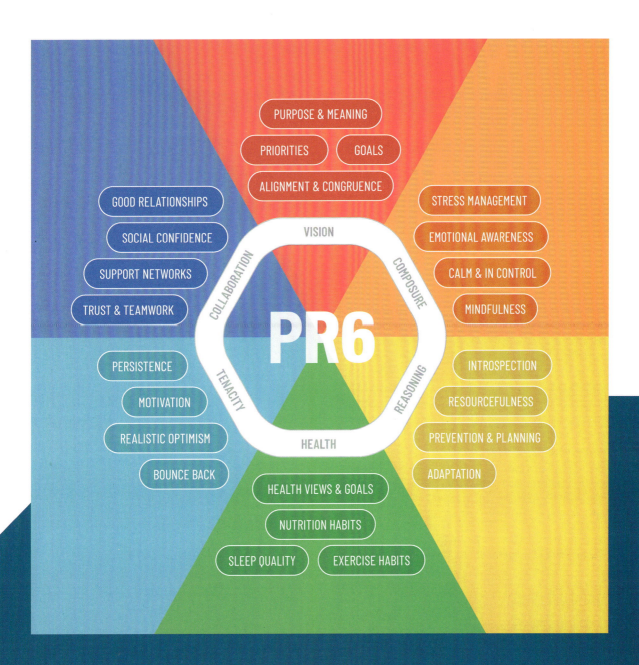

PURPOSE & MEANING
PRIORITIES   GOALS
ALIGNMENT & CONGRUENCE

GOOD RELATIONSHIPS
SOCIAL CONFIDENCE
SUPPORT NETWORKS
TRUST & TEAMWORK

STRESS MANAGEMENT
EMOTIONAL AWARENESS
CALM & IN CONTROL
MINDFULNESS

VISION
COLLABORATION   COMPOSURE

PR6

PERSISTENCE
MOTIVATION
REALISTIC OPTIMISM
BOUNCE BACK

TENACITY   REASONING
HEALTH

INTROSPECTION
RESOURCEFULNESS
PREVENTION & PLANNING
ADAPTATION

HEALTH VIEWS & GOALS
NUTRITION HABITS
SLEEP QUALITY   EXERCISE HABITS

Here we start to see how the domains link together, as Reasoning needs Vision for clarity of purpose and goals to drive decision-making, and it also needs Composure to keep the impulsive brain regulated and under control, so that the PFC can function at its best. All domains function together in this way to create the overall outcome of 'resilience': the way to advance and achieve our goals despite the adversity we face along the way.

In Reasoning, we'll explore **Sustainable Compartmenting, Optimizing Thoughts & Behaviors**, and **Concrete vs Abstract Processing**.

1.4.4   Health

Resilience is not simply a mental construct, but also has a physical component. Our own health affects how well we can deal with challenges in our path. Meanwhile, failing health can present the toughest challenge of all.

Good nutrition, quality sleep and exercise are all components of the Health domain.

Physical health in the past was rarely considered to be part of resilience. In fact, none of the major resilience measurement models included health as a domain of resilience. This is despite mounting evidence that shows how physical health influences mindset and coping abilities in multiple ways. The PR6 model includes health factors to establish a comprehensive mind-body model of resilience.

In the Health domain we'll explore skills around maintaining these important health factors while dealing with long hours and shift work in the Managing Work Hours module.

1.4.5 Tenacity

Optimism through adversity, persistence and bouncing back after disruptive events is what the Tenacity domain is about.

Very few of us get everything right the first time. Instead, the main quality that contributes to success is the willingness to be persistent. Even Einstein said, "It's not that I'm so smart, it's just that I stay with problems longer". Now, Einstein might have been bit smart as well, but the attitude is crucial. It's something worth paying extra attention to in a time of instant gratification. Our own willingness to remain hopeful despite setbacks and put consistent effort into relationships, friendships, work, investments, projects, and hobbies is what will eventually define our success. This is where Tenacity plays a key role in enabling the Vision domain.

In the Tenacity domain we'll explore two skills called **Mental Load Management** and **Three Good Things**.

1.4.6 Collaboration

Building healthy support networks, connecting with others, adapting to context, and managing perceptions is at the heart of our basic human need for connection with others. As the world becomes more complex, we need to be able to work more effectively with others to accomplish meaningful goals. This is especially true in organizations where cohesiveness of the workforce is crucial to building a healthy culture, a culture where people can support each other through turbulent change cycles and innovation. These are the key factors that make up the domain of Collaboration.

Connection with others is so important to us that the brain has developed specific areas to focus on this. Near the bottom of the brain on both sides sits the fusiform gyrus, which is specifically adapted to recognize facial expressions in other humans. It activates when we see the face of another person and produces a stronger reaction when that person is familiar to us. The brain also checks with the amygdala and memory centers to determine if there is any threat from this person. This affects the level of safety you feel around people.

Collaboration is a key domain within high adversity work. Here we'll explore four skills, called **High Quality Connections, Grief & Growth, Strong Relationships**, and **High Adversity Humor**

1.4.7 Foundational Skills

Each domain includes a set of foundational skills that can be learned through the standard Driven Resilience training. The HART program covers the more advanced skills of these domains that are useful for high adversity situations.

SCAN ME

Your HART Scores in the **Driven Resilience App**

Check your resilience and work survey scores in the **Driven Resilience App**. Scan the QR code below to explore (make sure you are **logged into the app** first).

app.hellodriven.com/activities/1247

ACTIVITY 1.4.1

Explore your domain strengths and opportunities. Use your PR6 Resilience Report if you have it available.

Vision Strengths

....
....
....
....
....
....
....

Vision Opportunities

....
....
....
....
....
....
....

Composure Strengths

....
....
....
....
....
....
....

Composure Opportunities

....
....
....
....
....
....
....

Reasoning Strengths

....
....
....
....
....
....
....

Reasoning Opportunities

....
....
....
....
....
....
....

ACTIVITY 1.4.1

Explore your domain strengths and opportunities. Use your PR6 Resilience Report if you have it available.

Health Strengths

◢..

◢..

◢..

◢..

◢..

◢..

◢..

Health Opportunities

◢..

◢..

◢..

◢..

◢..

◢..

◢..

Tenacity Strengths

◢..

◢..

◢..

◢..

◢..

◢..

◢..

Tenacity Opportunities

◢..

◢..

◢..

◢..

◢..

◢..

◢..

Collaboration Strengths

◢..

◢..

◢..

◢..

◢..

◢..

Collaboration Opportunities

◢..

◢..

◢..

◢..

◢..

◢..

NOTES

From the the **Work Survey Report**, write down 3 things going well, and 3 challenges to explore.

....

....

....

....

....

....

....

....

....

....

....

....

....

....

....

....

....

....

....

....

....

....

....

....

....

VISION

 **2.1**

CONNECTING
PURPOSE

2.1 CONNECTING PURPOSE

Learing Outcomes:

- Develop a sense of meaning and purpose
- Access a practical tool you can reflect on over time

This is Useful For:

- Staying motivated during tough times
- Finding appreciation for all aspects of your work

Out of all the different aspects of resilience, your **sense of purpose is the most important**. This is your Vision – the vision of your place in this world, the vision of you doing something meaningful.

When your purpose is clear and you are not held back or blocked from fulfilling your purpose, that's when you are at your best.

Thinking back to the three main aspects of challenges in high adversity work, resilience means being able to:

- Handle **operational** stress
- Negotiate **organizational** stress
- Manage **relational** stress

Building strength across how you can manage all three of these is what gives you **high adversity resilience**.

Managing all three of these factors takes some conscious effort. This is where it helps to see operational, organizational, and relational aspects not as obstacles, but as factors that enable you to live your purpose sustainably.

Being able to connect your purpose to these will help you build resilience through all the challenges you face. The Connected Purpose skill teaches you a way to achieve this.

2.1.1 Why Answer 'Why'?

'Why' is one of those questions we start to ask very early on as children. It's a question that helps us understand how the world works, why things are the way they are, and why we should do certain things.

Asking 'why' is an effort of the brain to help make sense of the world. This is one of the fundamental needs of the brain – the need to understand and have a clear idea of where we are going and to what end.

When this question of 'why' has no clear answer, then it can feel like the world just doesn't make sense. Later in life, not being able to answer 'why' can impact motivation. Think about these situations:

- You're struggling with something and think *"Why do I even bother?"*
- You have to complete a bunch of paperwork and think *"Why do I have to do this?"*
- Things keep going wrong and you think *"What's even the point of trying?"*

If your brain is silent when you think of these questions, then it can be hard to motivate yourself to complete the tasks you need to complete and keep going.

Why Did You Join?

Many people choosing high adversity occupations experience something of a 'calling' to this work. Officers joining the force to 'lock up bad guys'. Paramedics looking to save people. Firefighters wanting to battle structural fires. And so on.

Yet, for many the work turns out to be very different, and the 'why' for joining isn't really what they get to do. This can make it difficult to stay motivated over time, as your purpose becomes disconnected from the work and what you were hoping to achieve.

This happens to most people at some point in their careers, often early on. Being able to connect your 'why' to all the different parts of the work is helpful and important to be able to do the work sustainably. Think about the examples before:

- You're struggling with something and think *"This is hard, but I'll push through because I know why I'm doing this"*

- You have to complete a bunch of paperwork and think *"I know why I should do this paperwork. It's not my favorite part of the work, but it's still important."*
- Things keep going wrong and you think *"I know why I need to keep trying. This sucks, but I'll keep going"*

You can connect your 'why' to everything you need to do and use that to motivate yourself to get things done.

When you can do this well, you'll be able to turn the hardest parts of the work into tasks you take pride in and appreciate your ability to be disciplined and **find the value in everything you do**.

2.1.2   Happiness vs Meaning

A big misconception about life is that 'happiness' is the ultimate goal. For many people if you ask them what the meaning of their life is, they'd say it's "to be happy".

Happiness

Though, what is happiness?

- Happiness is a feeling of **joy and pleasure**
- It's **temporary**, often appearing for just an hour, or a few seconds
- It comes from **doing something else**
- It **doesn't motivate** you to do anything other than wanting to keep being happy

Certainly, it's nice to feel happy and the brain wants to feel happy. That's why it's something we often desire to have more of. Though the challenge with happiness is that **you can't get it by pursuing it directly**.

Happiness is similar to money – you can't get money by wanting more money – you must **do something** that earns money.

Same with happiness – you can't get happiness by wanting happiness – you need to do something else that produces happiness. Though there's a further challenge in happiness being temporary. No one is happy all the time, and that's ok. And since happiness isn't directly motivational, **it doesn't drive you to want to improve your life and the world**, since in that moment of happiness, life is great as it is.

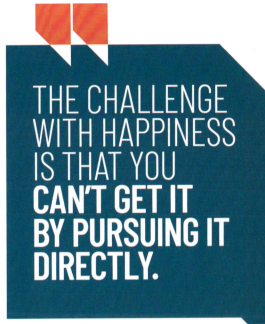

THE CHALLENGE WITH HAPPINESS IS THAT YOU CAN'T GET IT BY PURSUING IT DIRECTLY.

ACTIVITY 2.1.1

Have you found yourself in a situation like this, where the work turned out differently from what you were expecting?

....

....

....

....

....

....

....

....

....

....

....

Meaning

High adversity work is a good example of where happiness isn't the main goal. These are not jobs that are full of happy moments and fun. Working with people in their worst moments and wanting to reduce the suffering of others. Quite often it's just the opposite of happiness.

Instead, **high adversity work is more about 'meaning'**, which is much more important. What is the difference with meaning?

- Meaning is a feeling a **purpose and direction**
- It's **long-lasting** and can stay with you for a lifetime
- It is **your decision** of what you want to do
- It **breeds perseverance and motivates** you to keep growing and improve yourself and the world

After all, this is hard work, but we do it because it is meaningful and important.

As a result of pursuing your meaning and purpose, there will be moments of happiness. These are moments to fully enjoy and embrace, though happy moments are not the goal. The goal is to do something that matters to you.

It's this sense of meaning that is motivating in the long term and gets you through the times where there isn't a lot of happiness. It gives you pride in yourself and what you do and is something no one can ever take away from you.

2.1.3   Where to Find 'Why'

One of the toughest things about life is that it doesn't come with a nicely defined 'why'. It would be great if there was just one definite 'why' that everyone agrees on and that's why we all do what we do and we all work towards the same goal.

Unfortunately, that's not quite that case. This is where many people try to 'discover their purpose', or 'discover their passion'.

The problem again is that **purpose is often not something you discover**. The idea that you'll be going through life, and something will happen and suddenly you'll know what you're meant to be doing is not really how it works. Perhaps for some people this can happen, but for most of us, **purpose is a decision**.

This is where your purpose is something you decide and it might well come from the reason why you choose your career.

Somewhere in your life, you decide on your 'why' – you decide what is meaningful to you and why that is meaningful.

Hints: Try to keep it short and broad – something that you can pursue in many different ways. For example, "To help people", "To protect people" and so on are broad purpose statements that you can pursue in many different ways, giving you resilience to changes that might happen along the way.

ACTIVITY 2.1.2

What's your 'why'?

....
....
....
....
....
....
....
....
....
....
....
....
....
....

2.1.4 Four Circles of 'Why'

Having an idea of your purpose at a very high level allows you to now start connecting it to different concepts. Some of these might come easily, others maybe would need some thought. At the end you might even want to revise your idea of purpose – these are all useful parts of exploring these concepts.

This is where the four circles come in, surrounding the concept of 'Why'. This breaks down into four concepts:

- What you love or enjoy
- What you're good at
- What you can be paid for
- What the world needs

Each of these overlap as follows:

- Where what you love and what you're good at overlaps gives a feeling of **passion**
- Where what you love and what the world needs overlap gives a feeling of having a **mission**
- Where what you're good at and what you can get paid for overlaps is where you get a **profession**
- Where what the world needs and what you can get paid for overlaps is where you find a **vocation**

In the middle where they all overlap, that's where you find a powerful **why** – a strong sense of calling that this is where you need to be in the world.

2.1.5 Connecting to Each Circle

ACTIVITY 2.1.3

Often this concept is used to help people find their purpose. However, since you already have a chosen path in your life, we're going to flip this concept and use it to strengthen your purpose.

The way we'll do this is to **take the work you do and find parts of it that connect to each of the four circles**. You don't necessarily need to connect to each, but the more you can connect, the stronger your long-term motivation will likely be.

Now your challenge is to go through each of these four circles and see how you can connect parts of your work to each so that you can have solid connections.

Use the diagram to fill in each spot.

What Do You Love/Enjoy?

First up, let's look at what you love or enjoy. Here it's about finding aspects of your work that you genuinely enjoy doing. You don't need to be good at it, it's simply a part that you enjoy.

This could be about the people you work with, or a specific task you get to do.

What Are You're Good At?

Second, let's look at what you are good at. These might be things you don't necessarily enjoy, but you are good at performing the task itself.

As an example, some people were forced to practice the piano as children. This means as adults they are good at playing, but they don't necessarily enjoy it.

What Can You Be Paid For?

Money isn't necessarily a big motivator, but it helps to keep doing a specific job if you don't have to deal with financial worries because you're not getting paid, or not getting paid enough and need a second job which adds new challenges.

Of course, volunteering to help in communities is fantastic. Though still you'd need to be able to make a living to keep doing this in the long term.

Sometimes it also helps to have some kind of future that provides more financial security, such as knowing you can work your way up and achieve promotions.

What Does the World Need?

Lastly is to think about how your work is important to the world – how you are making the world a better place. Sometimes it can take a bit of stepping back and taking perspective on the broader impact of what you do, even if what you do is a small part of something much bigger.

The overall organization cannot function without each part working, and as a part of that you make an impact. Being able to connect some part of your work to why the world needs it is an important part of this exercise.

Write inside the circles for each part. Use the lines on the sides for any additional notes.

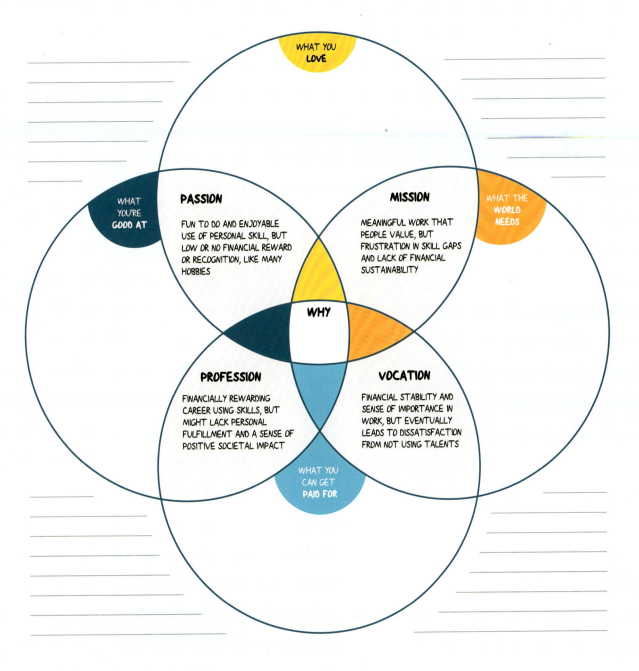

WHAT YOU
LOVE

WHAT
YOU'RE
GOOD AT

WHAT THE
WORLD
NEEDS

PASSION

FUN TO DO AND ENJOYABLE
USE OF PERSONAL SKILL, BUT
LOW OR NO FINANCIAL REWARD
OR RECOGNITION, LIKE MANY
HOBBIES

MISSION

MEANINGFUL WORK THAT
PEOPLE VALUE, BUT
FRUSTRATION IN SKILL GAPS
AND LACK OF FINANCIAL
SUSTAINABILITY

WHY

PROFESSION

FINANCIALLY REWARDING
CAREER USING SKILLS, BUT
MIGHT LACK PERSONAL
FULFILLMENT AND A SENSE OF
POSITIVE SOCIETAL IMPACT

VOCATION

FINANCIAL STABILITY AND
SENSE OF IMPORTANCE IN
WORK, BUT EVENTUALLY
LEADS TO DISSATISFACTION
FROM NOT USING TALENTS

WHAT YOU
CAN GET
PAID FOR

2.1.6 Connecting Purpose

For our last part about connecting purpose, let's look at a different angle. If you can master this technique, then you're well on your way to staying motivated even when things get tough.

You've now defined your purpose at a high level, and then connected it to the four circles. However, there are further connections to make. This is when you take all the other aspects of your work and **connect them together so you can see how they all relate to your purpose**.

In a way, it's like building a mental structure where you can see how it all fits together – everything you do fitting in with a larger organization that helps you do something meaningful in the world.

What You're Good At

Now try the same concept. Think of all the ways that the things that you are good at contribute and enable your purpose.

How does what you're good at directly connect to your purpose?

....

....

....

....

....

....

....

ACTIVITY 2.1.4

What You Love/Enjoy

Take what you wrote down here before and think further about how it connects.

> **Example from the author –** My purpose is to help people. Something I love to do is research. For me the connection is that the research I do helps me find better ways to improve people's lives, therefore what I love to do directly connects to my purpose!

How does what you love or enjoy as part of your work directly connect to your purpose?

....

....

....

....

It helps to write these out, as writing them solidifies this in your brain and helps you remember this when things are tough and you need some motivation.

The HART Certification

All the different types of training and exercises you do for your work also help contribute to your purpose.

This high adversity resilience training course is included in that. Thinking of ways in which this adds to your resilience in living your purpose will help you keep going through all the activities each day.

How can you connect your purpose to completing this training?

....

....

....

....

....

....

....

This training can help improve mental strength and persistence which could certainly help. It can give you techniques to enjoy your work more, and even enjoy the parts that you don't usually enjoy. It can help build better relationships that keep you motivated. It can give you ways to deal with the toughest parts of the job, helping you stay focused and do your best work with all the people you help and look after.

Overall, there are many ways to see how training like this, and all other training you do connect to your work and help improve your effectiveness.

The main challenge is to be willing and open to see how it all fits together so you can appreciate it.

Organizational Stress

Let's take a step back to the start where we talked about one of the big sources of stress. It's here where you can now also link your purpose to the different organizational stresses you might face.

For example – Lots of paperwork might feel tedious, but it's important to be able to keep proper track of what was done to minimize mistakes and improve quality control. Connecting purpose to this can change it from being a pain into feeling pride over your great record-keeping skills.

See if there are one of these examples you can pick from to connect your purpose to and try it out:

- Rigid internal procedures
- Tough training regimes
- Managing shift work
- Routine equipment or system maintenance
- Large volumes of paperwork
- Long work hours in crises
- Extreme time pressures

Try it out with one of those examples. How does that connect to your purpose?

....

....

....

....

....

....

....

....

If you can practice your mind to see the connection of tasks like those, **then they can change from a source of frustration into an appreciation for how it all works together to help you live your purpose within a larger organization**.

Of course, there are many things that you shouldn't just accept, like harassment, sexism, unfairness, and so on.

With these it's more a case of structural issues that need to be addressed. Here you can consider reporting the behavior and ask for help and push for improvements or seek justice for certain events.

Use your judgement along with the reporting and support structures to determine the right way forward with those situations.

2.1.7   Connect Purpose Wisely

Overall, this ability to connect your purpose to the tasks you need to do as part of your work and the different stresses you face is a powerful technique to stay motivated.

The key is to use this wisely, so you learn how to appreciate the things you need to, have the courage to call out what's wrong, and keep working toward creating a better future.

This applies to the rest of the resilience training as well. Use your judgement on which of the techniques can be useful across organizational, operational and relational factors. They all have their uses, and sometimes it just needs a bit of creative thinking.

As you make all these connections with your purpose, you are **making connections in your brain**.

These connections are what will help to keep you motivated through tough times, giving you a sense of deeper confidence and drive to handle both the larger and smaller challenges you'll face.

This means **you teach your brain to appreciate all the different things you need to do**.

So rather than the limbic brain activating when you have lots of paperwork to do, you teach your prefrontal cortex to calm down the limbic brain because you understand the importance of the task through its connection to your purpose.

From here, keep in mind to refer to the Connecting Purpose concept over time. Review the circles and how you're doing in each, and when you find yourself struggling with some aspect of the work, see if you can connect it to some part of the circles, which connects it back to your central 'Why'. Use this to give yourself the motivation to keep going.

SCAN ME

Connecting Purpose in the **Driven Resilience App**

Scan the link to access the skill in the app (make sure you are **logged into the app** first).

app.hellodriven.com/activities/1230

NOTES

HEALTH

3.1

MANAGING WORK HOURS

3.1 MANAGING WORK HOURS

Learing Outcomes:

- Learn about general challenges involved in working unusual hours
- Identify personal challenges around shift work & long hours
- Learn strategies to improve sleep, nutrition, exercise, and social connections

This is Useful For:

- Identifying strategies to improve management of work hours

There are all kinds of challenges with this type of work – from trouble getting enough sleep, to social disconnection, through to struggling with fatigue that can impact effectiveness when out on calls or doing other tasks.

Being able to maintain your physical and mental strength to effectively do your work is important. This means applying strategies to help manage the effects of shift work and long hours as efficiently as possible.

3.1.1 Health Impacts

The human body has evolved to be active during the day and rest at night. This means shift work and working unusual hours goes against the natural processes of the body. While society has come to depend on certain services being always available, we can't ignore the effects this can have. Research highlights increased longer-term risks such as:

- Cardiovascular disease
- High blood pressure
- Certain cancers
- Sleep disorders
- Mood disorders such as depression and anxiety

Given that high adversity occupations are dealing with the realities of life, it means that work needs to be done all hours of the day. With these things, it's not like an office job where the work will still be there the next day. Instead, here we generally have **time sensitive tasks** to be taken care of as soon as they appear. Naturally, this means that the job itself often involves shift work and long hours.

SCAN ME

QUICK TEST

Work Hours Check

Scan the code below to complete a short assessment to explore how you are currently experiencing the hours you work.

You can do this assessment again later to see how your skill changes over time. PS – make sure you are logged into your app to access this assessment.

app.hellodriven.com/activities/875

The most noticeable short-term effects include:

- Fatigue and 'jet lag'
- Sleepiness
- Insomnia
- Digestive troubles
- Irritability
- Reduced mental agility
- Reduced performance and efficiency

The shift work model in the graphic below has been suggested as the different pathways that lead to disease:

This model applies to any occupation where you might work long or unusual hours. But what does it mean?

Quite simply it means we must stay on top of four key components:

- Finding ways to get good quality sleep
- Keeping to a healthy diet and watching intake of alcohol and avoid smoking
- Keeping up with exercise
- Synchronize social connections

We'll look through all of these in the next few activities. However, some of these effects can be improved through shift rotation.

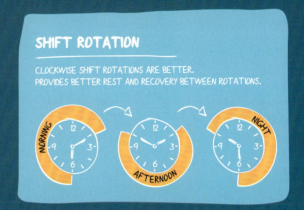

3.1.2 Effects of Shift Rotation

Researchers looking into the effects of different types of shift work found that a clockwise forward rotation of shifts led to less drowsiness and better work performance. A 5/2 shift rotation is an example.

Here you might work a morning shift for 5 days, rest 2 days, rotate to afternoon shift for 5 days, rest 2 days, rotate to night shift for 5 days, rest 2 days, and back to the start. Naturally, there is a lot of variation in shifts and work hours between occupations, so this part is mainly to illustrate the concept so that you can experiment and research what might work best for you.

Going counterclockwise (morning, to night, to afternoon) was found to be more draining and less effective. So, if there is a chance to schedule your work in this way, it could be worth a try.

This also leads to a broader thought, which is that different schedules work better for different people. Experimenting with different schedules and finding what works best for you is something worthwhile.

ACTIVITY 3.1.1

To what extent are these three needs met for you?

Need for control and orientation:

....
....
....
....
....
....

Need for connection:

....
....
....
....
....
....

Need for pleasure and avoidance of pain:

....
....
....
....
....
....

3.1.3 The Work-Life Balance Myth

An old yet popular idea is that there must be a balance between work and 'life'. This is often interpreted as something like 8 hours of work, 8 hours of leisure, and 8 hours of sleep.

While numerically that can look balanced, that's not quite how it works. Instead, for some people that still wouldn't feel balanced, while some can work very long hours and enjoy it.

The stress of work plays a significant role here.

For example: Perhaps you feel less stressed working a few extra hours because it allows you to work through things without being too rushed. This means working longer hours ends up being less stressful.

Most difficult, of course, is if you work very long hours and it's also extremely stressful all the way through.

This is where the concept of 'work-life balance' is a myth. What really enables you to sustainably work the hours you need to relate to meeting the **three basic needs of the brain**. These are:

- **The need for control and orientation –** This means you feel that your actions meaningfully contribute to your work, you know what you should be doing, and what you do is meaningful
- **The need for connection –** This means you have high quality connections with the people you work with, fulfilling the very basic need of the brain to have meaningful relationships
- **The need for pleasure and avoidance of pain –** Quite simply, this means you do things you enjoy and don't have to do too many things that you genuinely dislike

These are very fundamental human needs, and these combine to build self-esteem. What does this mean? It means you can work 20 hours a week at one job, but you have no friends there and you do stuff you really dislike, so you'll still feel like the work is draining.

Or you can work 60 hours a week at another job, but your work is meaningful, you work with great people, and you get to do stuff you're skilled at and enjoy. And even though it's long hours, afterwards you still feel energized and that it was worth it. **This is the difference it makes when you meet your basic needs.**

Here it becomes clearer that it's not about the hours, but more about the quality of the work environment.

ACTIVITY 3.1.2

Consider these sleep challenges and ways to improve sleep in the future.

Sleep Quality

The guideline for adults is to get around 7 to 9 hours of sleep each night. A key part of sleep is to know that **quality matters**. An hour of quality sleep is very different from an hour of low-quality sleep.

That is why you might be getting enough hours, but still feel tired when you wake up. Let's look at some specific challenges you might face, and ways you can manage them:

☐ Sleeping when the sun is out

Long hours and late shifts often mean getting home and having to sleep while the sun is out. However, any bit of light that makes it into your room reduces sleep quality as the light still goes through your eyelids when closed.

Invest in blackout curtains, or otherwise get a good quality eye mask that doesn't put pressure on your eyes. If none of those are available, use a cloth or some clothing to cover your eyes and block out any light.

☐ People trying to contact you

A difficult part of sleeping during the day is that everyone else is awake and going about their business. This means you are likely to get more calls and notifications.

Remember to set your phone and other devices to be fully silent – a phone vibrating on the table next to you can still wake you up. If needed, phones usually have some ways to allow certain people to contact you in case of emergency.

☐ Ambient noise

When everyone else is awake, they also tend to make much more noise. This noise also reduces sleep quality.

If there are noises keeping you awake you can try things like a white noise machine or app, or noise-cancelling earphones to block more sounds, or even simple earplugs to get better sleep.

☐ Caffeine and stimulants

Late work and shifts often mean resorting to coffee or energy drinks to keep you awake for those last few hours. The trouble is that caffeine 6 hours before sleep time reduces sleep quality by about 1 hour.

Limit caffeine intake to your last drink about 6 hours before you'll be going to sleep.

☐ Trouble falling asleep

If you've had a very active or difficult day, it can be hard to fall asleep. Being able to calm a racing mind takes practice and sometimes this can be especially difficult.

You can try a sleep meditation specifically designed to help you relax your mind and fall asleep. You can also try sleep sounds to play in the background. For some these are very helpful. In the Driven Resilience App Explore menu under Sleep you can find some of these.

☐ Sleep aids & alcohol

Sometimes we might get into a habit of using stimulants to stay awake and then use sleep drugs or even alcohol to fall asleep. The trouble here is that frequent use of sleep medication can also lead to lower quality sleep. Same for alcohol – it might get you to sleep faster, but sleep quality is reduced. Meaning you get the hours, but don't feel as refreshed.

As far as possible, try to avoid using sleep medication or alcohol as a sleep aid.

ACTIVITY 3.1.2 *cont.*

What challenges do you face with your sleep schedules?

....
....
....
....
....

What has helped you manage these challenges?

....
....
....
....
....

What new strategies can you try?

....
....
....
....
....
....

3.1.4 Sleep Strategies

Shift work and long hours tend to affect sleeping patterns the most.

This is worthwhile exploring since sleep is an absolute necessity for you to effectively do your work and simply function as a person. **Sleep deprivation** has a long list of negative effects, including:

- Memory lapses
- Irritability, short temper
- Involuntary microsleeps
- Reduced reaction time
- Reduced cognitive function
- More accident-prone

Interestingly, after a few days of sleep deprivation, the brain starts to force some areas of the brain to go to 'sleep'. This creates all kinds of strange effects, like hallucinations, loss of senses, and so on. Overall, sleep is crucial, which means you should prioritize this as something to manage.

Get your sleep checked

If you feel like you've already tried everything but still struggle with sleep, then there could be something else going on.

For example:

- **Obstructive sleep apnea** (sometimes called 'heroic snoring') is about the airways being obstructed to such a degree that it increases the risk of stroke or heart disease. It manifests as extremely loud snoring
- **Insomnia** is a complex sleep disorder with many potential causes. Between 10% and 30% of adults develop insomnia at some point in their lives, but there are ways to manage it
- **Nightmares and night terrors** cause sleep disruptions through the night, resulting in less quality sleep and difficulty getting back to sleep
- **Stress** is a common enemy of quality sleep. You can have the best sleep space in the world and stress can still make it impossible to enjoy it. If your mind won't stop, try some meditations, or address the source of the stress

If you are unsure what's causing difficulty in sleep, seeing a specialist can help to find out what's happening. Otherwise, if you know it's stress or nightmares, seeing a therapist can help. Get a referral from your doctor if you feel this might be the case.

ACTIVITY 3.1.3

Consider the task of staying awake and alert.

Staying Awake

Getting quality sleep is important, but so is staying awake and mentally sharp during your work hours.

☐ **Light exercise**

A quick walk around to get your blood moving and heartbeat faster can help if you're feeling drowsy. Light exercise tends to work better than a heavy workout, which could make you feel even more tired afterwards.

☐ **Caffeine**

Hey, it works! As before, just try to not have coffee or energy drinks too close to when you will be going to sleep.

☐ **Strategic napping**

The US Army recently added naps to the Holistic Health and Fitness manual as a strategy to increase alertness. There's been much research on this over the years, showing about 10 to 20 minutes is best. Longer than that, and you might wake up groggy as that's when you start to go into deep sleep.

☐ **Rocket nap**

Why not combine caffeine and a nap? Research shows that the combination is better than the sum of the parts. It's simple – drink a cup of coffee, then immediately take a 20-minute nap. Also known as a coffee nap, this is a quick and proven way to boost energy and attention for long hours and shifts.

☐ **More small meals**

Large and heavy meals tend to take a lot of energy to digest and can leave you tired. That's why breaking meals into smaller and lighter portions can help you stay awake more easily.

☐ **Talk to people**

Having conversations with co-workers helps to keep the brain stimulated, especially at times when you are usually drowsier. Bringing in humor can be especially useful in these times.

What strategies have helped you to stay awake and alert?

◢ ....

◢ ....

◢ ....

◢ ....

◢ ....

What new strategies can you try?

◢ ....

◢ ....

◢ ....

◢ ....

◢ ....

SCAN ME

TECHNIQUE

Sleep Meditation

Need help falling asleep? Try scanning the code below to use a step-by-step sleep meditation to help.

You can do this assessment again later to see how your skill changes over time. PS – make sure you are **logged into your app** to access this assessment.

app.hellodriven.com/activities/510

3.1.5 Nutrition & Exercise

Beyond sleep, work hours often affect two other areas important for good health and wellbeing, namely good nutrition and regular exercise.

Healthy Nutrition

Let's consider quickly what is 'healthy nutrition' in the first place. At a basic level it means:

- Eating more whole foods and less processed foods
- Eating lots of non-starchy vegetables
- Aoiding sugars and high-carbohydrate foods & drinks

However, working shifts and long hours can make eating healthy meals difficult. Some common nutrition challenges include:

- Not having the time to eat or make healthy meals every day
- Eating at irregular times
- Eating more fast food since it's quick and easy
- Having more cravings for unhealthy food due to lack of sleep
- Stomach issues are reported by people working shifts and irregular hours

Nutrition Tips

Eating More Whole Foods and Less Processed Foods

Incorporating more whole foods into your diet means prioritizing fresh, unprocessed, or minimally processed items, including fruits, vegetables, lean protein sources like meats, nuts, and seeds. This shift is essential because whole foods retain more of their natural nutrients, including vitamins, minerals, and fiber, which can sometimes be lost during the processing phase.

Importantly, whole foods generally contain fewer artificial additives and preservatives commonly found in processed foods. Reducing your intake of processed foods can potentially lower the risk of developing various health issues, including obesity and heart diseases, fostering a healthier digestive system, and promoting overall wellbeing.

Eating Lots of Non-Starchy Vegetables

Non-starchy vegetables like leafy greens, carrots, broccoli, and cauliflower are typically low in calories and carbohydrates but rich in essential nutrients such as vitamins, minerals, and dietary fiber. These vegetables can help in maintaining a healthy weight as they promote a feeling of fullness with fewer calories.

They have a lower glycemic index compared to starchy vegetables, which means they have a less significant impact on blood sugar levels. This can be especially beneficial in managing and preventing conditions like diabetes. Including a variety of non-starchy vegetables in your diet can also aid in fostering a diverse and healthy gut microbiome, promoting digestive health.

Avoiding Sugars and High-Carbohydrate Foods & Drinks

High intake of sugars and high-carbohydrate foods can lead to a spike in blood sugar levels, potentially resulting in increased insulin resistance, a precursor to type 2 diabetes. Furthermore, consuming sugary foods and drinks often can contribute to weight gain and obesity, which are risk factors for several other health conditions, including heart disease and certain cancers.

Excess sugar can also lead to dental issues like cavities and tooth decay. By limiting your intake of sugars and high-carbohydrate foods, you can help manage your weight better and prevent various health complications. Opting for complex carbohydrates like whole grains, which release energy slowly and help in maintaining sustained energy levels, can be a healthier choice.

ACTIVITY 3.1.4

Consider how you can maintain healthy eating habits.

Here are some ways that shift workers have found to manage these challenges.

☐ **Plan your meals**

Planning when to eat so you can fit meals into a regular schedule that works alongside meals before and after work can help make sure you eat regularly. You can set alarms to help remind you when to eat if you tend to miss meals.

☐ **Bulk meal prep**

If you have little time, it can be much more efficient to do one big cooking session each week to prepare healthy meals in bulk. That means you have all your food ready for the week and simply grab a few containers from the fridge or freezer for each workday. There are lots of bulk recipes out there that can help you stay healthy even if you have little time.

☐ **More small meals**

This was mentioned in the sleep section as well. The key point is to plan for smaller meals as this can help with digestion and reduce the effect of large meals causing drowsiness.

☐ **Get snacked up**

Stocking up on healthy snacks can help keep you awake and help to avoid resorting to fast foods and unhealthy snacks. Fruit and vegetable snacks are much better than grabbing candy bars and chips. Nuts or low-carb protein bars can be helpful for these times if you need something with a longer expiry date.

☐ **Get a craving stopper**

Struggle with cravings? Keep something like sugar free mints or chewing gum around to avoid giving in to cravings for something unhealthy.

Contingency planning

If there's a chance you'll get called away and miss meals, then it's time to get smart with planning ahead. This could mean:

☐ **Hiding snacks** in different places so that you've got something to eat even if you must run off somewhere

☐ **Keeping snacks** in foil or a plastic bag can help to quickly wrap them, so they won't spoil until you're back

☐ **Recruiting people** to your mission and telling them to help keep you on track with eating well

With some clever planning you can make sure you always eat healthy foods at a reasonable time.

☐ **Don't get dehydrated**

It's easy to get so focused on a task that you forget to drink water. This can cause headaches and muscle pains eventually. Keep a water bottle in sight to help remind you to drink. And if it's difficult to remember, set a reminder on your phone!

What strategies have helped you with nutrition?

....
....
....
....
....

What new strategies can you try?

....
....
....
....
....

ACTIVITY 3.1.5

A way to motivate yourself to exercise and also choose the right type of workout plan is to make two lists.

Passion – Write down a few types of workouts that you enjoy (e.g. weightlifting, dancing, hiking...)

◢...

◢...

◢...

◢...

◢...

◢...

◢...

Purpose – Next, set out which types of workouts could help your work. Essentially, which type of workout will help you fulfil your purpose?

◢...

◢...

◢...

◢...

◢...

◢...

◢...

◢...

Compare the lists and see which exercise type fits best across both passion and purpose and try that. This will help give you more motivation to do the workout and keep doing it.

Regular Exercise

The **best type of exercise is that which you will keep doing** so you have long-term fitness and health.

This is worth keeping in mind, as working long hours or shift work can often leave you feeling drained with little energy to exercise. Lack of sleep can also make it hard to take on a gym session.

Still, fitness is an important part of health, and often a requirement for many frontline occupations due to physical demands. This is also important not just for your body, but your brain as well.

THE BEST TYPE OF EXERCISE IS THAT WHICH **YOU WILL KEEP DOING.**

ACTIVITY 3.1.6

Think about your experience so far with exercise.

Below are more ideas on how you can stay consistent with exercise.

☐ **Gain without pain**

not entirely true. You don't need to demolish yourself in the gym to be able to benefit from working out.

Even just going for a walk is already helpful. Add in some squats, push-ups and a few planks and you already have a workout going without it feeling like punishment.

Of course, if your job requires extreme fitness, then it might be different. Though for the most part just pushing yourself a little bit more each time is all you really need to progress.

☐ **Go for hyper efficiency**

Staying fit doesn't mean you need to work out for a full hour every day. If you are very short on time, look for more efficient workouts, such as High Intensity Interval Training (HIIT). These workouts tend to last between 15 and 20 minutes and have been shown to raise heart rate and burn fat for 24 hours afterwards.

You can get even more efficient by setting yourself up to do these at home or in the workplace itself, removing the time it would take to go to a gym.

Doing just four of these sessions in a week can already make a huge contribution to staying physically fit and healthy.

☐ **Get a partner**

Research shows one of the most reliable ways to stick to work out plans is to get someone to exercise with. Even if this is a trainer, having someone else to keep you accountable is a great way to stay motivated.

☐ **Schedule & go early**

Schedule specific times for your workouts and try to do it earlier in the day to get it out of the way. You're much more likely to skip a workout if it's at the end of a long day or shift.

☐ **Small steps for big discipline**

Exercise is easy to avoid when it feels like a big thing is to be done. For example, if it means packing gear, putting on workout clothes, getting on public transport to get there, etc. Then it can feel like so much effort.

This is where setting it up to be super easy and simple to start can help you maintain much more discipline. For example, rather than thinking about doing a whole big workout, think instead *"I'm going to do 5 bodyweight squats right now in my current clothes."*

Then you'd probably notice that was easy, so you decide to do some more, and some more. And maybe get into different clothes and start working out a bit harder. Next thing you know, you might have done a full workout.

What has helped you in the past with sticking to a fitness routine?

....

....

....

....

....

What new strategies can you try to work out and stay consistent?

....

....

....

....

....

3.1.6 Social Connections

One area that's often neglected in high adversity occupations is connection with people that you don't work with. That means friends, family, partners, children, and so on.

Maintaining social connections can be more difficult when working long hours and shifts. Some challenges here include:

- ◢ Little time available for **loved ones**
- ◢ Missing out on **social gatherings**
- ◢ Missing **important moments** in other people's lives
- ◢ Drifting apart from **old friendships**
- ◢ Difficulty aligning chores & other **housework responsibilities**
- ◢ Even coming back from a long shift can take an extra day of sleep to **catch up and be functional again**, leaving even less time to really connect with people.

Let's go through some ideas that could help with maintaining meaningful connections, despite difficult schedules.

ACTIVITY 3.1.7

Think about how you're doing with social connections in relation to the hours you work.

Make the most of time at home

When you have little time to spend with others, one of the most important things is to put extra effort into making the most of the time you do have with people.

This is where the Compartmenting skill can come in to help you stay focused and present in the moment so you can really connect during these times while still working through stress and other challenges when it works best. Some ideas:

☐ If you're in a relationship, **take extra time** with your partner to say goodbye and to welcome each other home. You might not get a lot of time together, so this simple change to spend a bit longer in a hug before leaving and when coming home can help set the tone for the day and constantly re-affirm your affection for each other

☐ **Make mealtimes a time for everyone** to catch up, putting phones away and minimizing outside distractions

☐ **Take time to schedule** activities and things to do on weekends or days that you do have off. Even if it's something simple, this can help create some quality time that might otherwise just fly by if nothing is planned

When time is scarce, put in extra effort to make the most of it!

Communicate and schedule

Talk to people about the nature of your work and how your schedule works. Clear communication is important here, so everyone understands your situation and how to fit into it. For example:

☐ If you work shifts, **explain these to people** so they know when you are available and when you aren't

Make more work friends

work with that you can most easily socialize with.

Trying to build relationships with people in the general public can be difficult. Often, they might not understand the pressures of the work, and even just finding time to meet can be difficult as they don't fit in with shifts and hours.

While that doesn't mean you should avoid building relationships with people outside your work, it does mean it can be easier to build closer connections with those you work with.

This could mean planning get-togethers and trying to say hello and get to know people. They're likely in the same situation that you are, so you might find them more open to connect.

Use social networks wisely

Social networks can be useful to stay in touch and share important moments in the lives of friends and family. However, keep in mind that social networks can also bring negative feelings due to not being able to participate in those events and subconscious social comparison.

If you choose to use social networks to stay in touch, only do so to the degree that you feel it's something positive in your life. If you feel it's starting to impact you negatively, then it might be time to take a break from it.

Otherwise, use technology for the things it's good for – staying in touch and connected. Try to ask people how they're doing. Find out what's been happening in their lives. Tell them about what's been happening with you

Making a conscious effort to maintain and build relationships can be challenging when your energy is already drained. However, this is crucial to long term wellbeing to maintain meaningful relationships, giving you more reason to keep doing what is meaningful to you.

That's it for work hours and schedules. There are lots of ways to manage the impacts of long shifts and hours, and the main thing is to make a conscious effort to manage these well.

Doing so will help you stay effective in your work while also having the energy to really enjoy your time away from work.

What has helped you in the past with sticking to a fitness routine?

....

....

....

....

....

What new strategies can you try to work out and stay consistent?

....

....

....

....

....

SCAN ME

Managing Work Hours in the Driven Resilience App

Scan the link to access the skill in the app (make sure you are **logged into the app** first).

app.hellodriven.com/activities/1231

NOTES

REASONING

4.1
SUSTAINABLE COMPARTMENTING

4.1 SUSTAINABLE COMPARTMENTING

Learing Outcomes:

- Learn a set of practical tools manage the impact of high stress events in different parts of life
- Learn how to create compartments, manage them, and recognize overflow
- Learn how to use compartmenting to enhance communication skills
- Understand stepped self-care

This is Useful For:

- Developing mental discipline to stay focused and be effective despite facing other challenges
- Becoming better at talking about challenges you face

The nature of high adversity work is that its importance means it often leaves us thinking about it all hours of the day. An incident or some event can linger on for a long time after work, affecting the rest of the day.

4.1.1   What is Compartmenting?

To help understand what it is, consider this - do you ever spend time with friends, family, or your children, and just can't stop thinking about something that happened at work? Or some work problem you need to solve?

When this happens, your time with people you care about is compromised.

You don't enjoy yourself as much, and the people you're with often notice something's wrong, even if they don't say anything.

Of course, this also affects your own time when you're by yourself. Not being able to switch off can lead to constant worry. In extreme cases, these can escalate and add towards feelings of anxiety or depression.

What you ideally should be able to do is:

- When you're with someone, have the ability to **be fully present and enjoy the moment** without your mindset being clouded by other things
- When you're by yourself, have the ability to **choose to switch off and fully enjoy something** without worry, guilt or other emotions bothering you

SCAN ME

QUICK TEST

Compartmenting Skill Check

Scan the code below to complete a short assessment of your current compartmenting skill. You can do this assessment again later to see how your skill changes over time. PS – make sure you are logged into your app to access this assessment.

app.hellodriven.com/activities/780

This is where compartmenting as an advanced resilience skill is especially useful for managing a high stress job.

You might also notice here that, in a way, this crosses over with mindfulness. It helps you be present in the moment without being burdened by things you'd rather put aside for a while.

What it's not

Still, there are different types of compartmenting –
some that are helpful, and some that are not. For
example:

- ◢ This is not a way to avoid problems you should be
  managing
- ◢ It's not a way to avoid managing the emotional
  impact of a difficult experience
- ◢ This is not a way to avoid dealing with
  contradictions in your beliefs and behaviors
- ◢ It's not about developing split personalities so that
  you are different people in different situations

These above are examples of **subconscious**
compartmenting, where the brain uses it as a defense
mechanism to protect itself from experiencing difficult
emotions or facing difficult realities. Therefore, it's
important to learn about this in more detail to develop
what we call **Sustainable Compartmenting**.

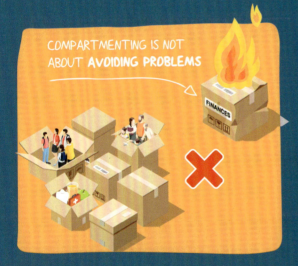

COMPARTMENTING IS NOT
ABOUT **AVOIDING PROBLEMS**

Sustainability means developing mental discipline to
master your subconscious mind. This gives you a way
to sustainably do high stress work while processing
events effectively at the right time and allows you to
unwind quickly so you can enjoy your time away from
work.

NOTES

THE EXTREME OPPOSITE OF COMPARTMENTING IS GENERALIZING.

This kind of change in behavior can happen to anyone, and it's often after years of service that some unexpected event just stands out from the rest.

The challenge for Jim here is that he's doing the extreme opposite of compartmenting, which is **generalizing**. He generalizes that, because he has seen this happen, it means it can happen again at any time. And even if the chance of it happening is remote, it's so horrific when it happens that he needs to do everything he can to avoid it.

This kind of thinking mainly comes from the limbic brain, producing a strong fearful reaction and memory that influences behavior, even though it's not entirely logical.

NOTES

....

....

....

....

....

....

....

....

....

....

....

....

....

....

....

EXAMPLE

Jim's Extreme Experience

To help you think about this more, consider Jim's experience and his actions.

Jim is an EMT and gets called to a mass casualty shooting – something that rarely happens in his region. When he gets there, police are securing the area and the air is filled with screams of injured people and those of people with them. Even though he's been an EMT for years, this is the first time he's seen an event of this scale.

After triage, he helps to transport a young girl in critical condition to the hospital, separating her from her mother at the scene.

Later that night, he can't stop thinking about the chaos of the scene - the screams of her mother, the pain in the young girl's eyes and her muffled murmurs as she struggled with a chest wound.

Jim thinks to himself:

"The world is a dangerous place. I've seen now how quickly it can happen. I've seen the pain and suffering and death that can happen. I can't afford to relax around my son and partner."

"I could never forgive myself if something happened to them and I wasn't paying attention – if I wasn't there or ready to protect them."

Jim feels that he must make this sacrifice, to give up his own happiness and wellbeing so that he can always be vigilant and protect his family.

What's the effect of this?

- When he's with his family he's always on edge and doesn't let himself relax

- He's overly protective, resulting in a short temper and snapping at his partner or son when they do something remotely dangerous

- He's always concerned with what is going on around him, resulting in not really listening to what his family is saying

- Over time it puts a strain on his marriage, with his partner feeling like Jim doesn't really pay attention to her, but Jim feels that he's already making a big sacrifice to keep the family safe and is only trying to protect them

- Meanwhile his son is starting to resent Jim because of not being allowed enough freedom to live and have fun like the other kids, slowly driving a wedge between them

It's not a good or healthy situation, but unfortunately this happens often.

A Better Approach?

Let's explore what could have helped here.

When Jim went through his experience, he could have quickly put that event into his Work compartment – taking a step back to recognize that these are the kind of rare challenges he deals with in his work.

Within that mindset, he can apply his understanding of risk in relation to his work.

What does this mean? Quite simply it means that he knows that his job is to deal with extreme events, but these events are rare in everyday life.

Therefore, he understands that his experiences at work **don't need to change who he is outside of work**. He can still relax. He can still have fun and laugh. He can still let other people have their own freedom and make their own mistakes.

Jim's Advantage

The advantage here is that he is **happier with his family and when he has time by himself**. This gives him the space and supportive environment to find the energy to process his experience and keep going with renewed drive and motivation.

Effectively, compartmenting that experience helps preserve the integrity of his other compartments, which helps him process the experience faster with less disruption in his life.

This is effectively what compartmenting is – a system to process stress in one area of your life, while preserving the integrity of other areas.

Within this process is the 'virtuous circle' – a concept showing that the areas you protect **can become the energy source to manage stress and difficult experiences** in more challenging areas. This motivates you to keep going and continue to get value from your work.

Why Use Compartments?

Here are a few more reasons for why compartmenting is important:

- If you don't use compartments, it's easy for **problems in one area of your life to affect other areas** and people in your life, like taking work stress out on your partner
- This can **lead to new problems that make things even worse** (like relationship issues, difficulty sleeping, mood swings, financial issues), and make it hard to find and solve the real issue
- Compartmenting **gives you time and space** to properly process high stress events and problems
- It gives you the **tools and mental clarity to communicate** with people close to you about the biggest challenges you face
- It allows you to **have confidence in your ability** to deal with difficult situations so you can sustainably thrive in your career, while protecting other areas of your life from unnecessary overflow

As we go through this course, you'll notice some interesting mental challenges to make sure you stick to healthy purposeful compartmenting, while learning to avoid subconscious habits and reactions.

> COMPARTMENTING IS A SYSTEM TO **PROCESS STRESS** IN ONE AREA OF YOUR LIFE, WHILE **PRESERVING THE INGETRITY OF OTHER AREAS.**

ACTIVITY 4.1.1

Have you experienced this yourself, where things that happened at work affected your view of the world?

....
....
....
....
....
....
....
....
....
....
....
....
....
....
....
....
....
....
....
....
....
....

4.1.2   Organizing Compartments

Now that we have an idea of what compartmenting is, let's look at more practical stuff.

A good place to start is by exploring some examples of compartments.

One of the most obvious examples of a compartment is "Work", so what other ones might there be? Here is list a few examples, keeping in mind that yours could be different.

- **Friends** – Anything from close friends to those you don't see often (or ever!)
- **Family** – Including immediate family and extended
- **Partner** – If you have a life partner it's useful to separate them from others, since you have a special bond as people that chose each other to share a life. Taking special precautions to protect this relationship is important. Even children who bring new pressures and challenges still shouldn't override you and your partner caring for each other
- **Hobbies** – All the activities you like to do for recreation
- **Health** – Your physical health, including sleep, nutrition, exercise, and everything else happening with your body physically
- **Finances** – Anything from income, to savings, investments, debt, and so on

Those are some of the common ones, though of course yours might look very different.

EXAMPLES OF **COMPARTMENTS**

Now you might wonder: *"Doesn't everyone have these boxes anyway?"*

In some way, yes, most people do create these at a subconscious level, but here's the difference – when you have these boxes by default, **an issue in one usually overflows to others**.

For example:

- Having a fight with a friend might make you brood around your partner, not enjoy your hobbies for a while, be distracted at work, and so on
- Sustainable conscious compartmenting would put in place the mental discipline to deal with this situation (fighting with a friend) at the right time, without letting it affect your work, hobbies, and partner unnecessarily

Let's illustrate:

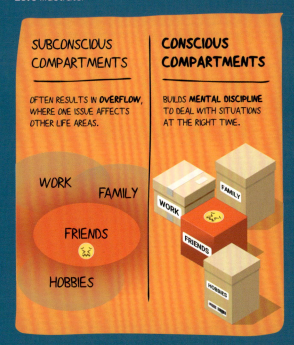

With compartmenting **you can visualize** yourself putting that fight in the Friend box, pushing it to the side for now, opening up the Hobbies box, and doing something you enjoy without being preoccupied with the friend stuff for now.

That's the difference!

Of course, not everything needs to be compartmented. You can focus on doing this with the main aspects of life to help keep your mind organized.

ACTIVITY 4.1.2

What kind of compartments might you have?

....
....
....
....
....
....
....
....
....
....
....
....
....
....
....
....
....
....
....
....
....
....
....

....
....
....
....
....
....
....
....
....
....
....
....
....
....
....

Here are some interesting effects of having a separate box for 'Me':

◿ Since **finances** is a separate box, having more or less money, or having financial issues doesn't affect who you are or your self-worth as a person

◿ Since **health** is separate, getting injured, sick, or even losing limbs doesn't change who you are. Even something like chronic pain is something in this compartment, and doesn't necessarily change 'you'

◿ With **work** being separate, helping people through extreme situations doesn't have to change you as a person that perhaps likes to just have fun and enjoy life outside of work

This is a good example of a high degree of resilience, where things happening in each of these boxes don't affect you at your core. It means you remain confident and centered in yourself, while managing whatever situation you face in another area of your life.

Still, this doesn't mean the other boxes aren't also important...

The 'Me' Box

There's another very important box we haven't mentioned yet. This is the 'Me' box, which is about **the type of person you are and your core values**.

Don't Overdo It

Something to check for is overdoing the number of compartments, where things are broken down into very small groups.

While there can be advantages to this, it also tends to make life really complicated – more complicated than it needs to be. This can take a lot of mental effort to keep organized.

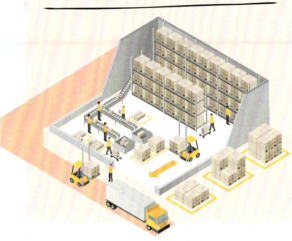

LOTS OF BOXES CAN BE TOO COMPLICATED

Also, Check the Size

Considering how much time and mental power goes into the different areas of your life, what would your picture look like?

ONE AREA **DOMINATING ALL OTHERS?**

CONSIDER IF IT WORKS FOR YOU AND IS MEANINGFUL, OR IF A DIFFERENT BALANCE CAN HELP.

WORK

FINANCES · FAMILY · FRIENDS · HEALTH · ME

ACTIVITY 4.1.3

Do you have an area that dominates all others? Does it work for you?

....
....
....
....
....
....
....
....
....
....
....

There's no right answer here with what it should look like. For some it might be fine for the Work box to be very big if they feel it's meaningful and important to them, and that those close to them understand this choice.

How Compartmenting Works

Now we have some ideas of compartments, but how does it actually work? Just like when you move house, simply labelling boxes doesn't automatically make your household objects go into them – **you need to do some packing**.

The outcome you're looking for here is to be able to quickly move from one compartment to the other and fully focus your attention where you want. In real terms, this can mean that when you head home from work, **you leave work at work** and can fully engage with your family and friends.

For some people, this can develop to a point where they totally forget about work until the next day and must look at their emails to remember what they were even doing the day before! That means outside of work, they are **totally free and unburdened and can fully relax**, which ends up making them feel happier at work and perform better.

....
....
....
....
....
....
....
....
....
....
....
....
....
....
....
....
....
....
....
....
....
....

Catch and Pause

The basic concept of how this works sounds simple enough – you put stuff from your life into relevant boxes. Still, it's not as simple as saying *"I won't let work things affect my home life"*.

To actually do this requires a quick mindfulness exercise to practice over and over, each time you find yourself being preoccupied about something at work.

This is the catch and pause exercise, which works like this:

When you catch yourself being preoccupied with something from work, pause to visualize:

- **Visualize** your compartments
- **Notice** something from one box is trying to get to another where it shouldn't be (like an issue at work is interfering with you relaxing at home)

Now visualize picking up that object, and ask:

- Do I need to **deal with this** right now?
- Am I going to **solve this** right now?
- Is this **helpful** to think about right now?

If the answer is *"No"* to these questions, visualize putting the object back in its proper place, close that box, and focus on what you actually want to.

NOTICE SOMETHING **OUT OF PLACE?**

1. **VISUALISE** COMPARTMENTS
2. **CATCH** WHAT IS OUT OF PLACE & **PAUSE**
3. **CONSIDER** IF IT'S HELPFUL, OR IF IT SHOULD BE SENT BACK

Through constantly practicing catch and pause you start to develop the mental discipline to keep things where they should be, allowing you to focus and relax when you want.

EXAMPLE

Jim's Board Game

To help you think about this more, consider Jim's Jim is playing a board game with his family. They're all laughing and enjoying themselves

Unexpectedly, the dice hitting the board in the game reminds Jim of something that happened a while ago

Jim starts thinking about this and goes quiet. His family senses something's wrong, the laughter quiets down and they keep playing in silence. His wife gives him a concerned look

At this point, Jim **catches** that work is intruding into family time. He **pauses** and realizes it's not helpful right now to think about this as it's affecting the quality of their family time

He visualizes the boxes, put the work stuff back where it should be, and says *"Hmm... was just thinking about something that happened at work"*. Looking at his wife he says: *"I'll tell you about it later"*. Turns back to the family: *"Anyway, where were we!"* And gets back into the game and enjoys the moment.

SCAN ME

TECHNIQUE

Catch & Pause for Compartmenting

Scan the code below to use a step-by-step Catch & Pause technique to help with compartmenting in the Driven Resilience App.

PS – make sure you are **logged into your app** to access this technique.

app.hellodriven.com/activities/1024

ACTIVITY 4.1.4

Catch & Pause – where can this be helpful for you?

....
....
....
....
....
....
....
....
....
....
....
....
....
....
....
....
....

Important - This doesn't mean you aren't allowed to talk about work things when you're not at work. In fact, it's just the opposite.

Compartmenting can help you **communicate about what's happening at work or elsewhere more effectively**.

It also doesn't mean problems are supposed to be boxed away and avoided. Again, it's just the opposite. This is about giving you the mental space to focus on where you are, and then deal with challenges at the right time to be most effective. After all, challenges and problems always need to be managed and taken care of to stay on top of life.

4.1.3 Understanding Overflow

To be present in the moment, we might be putting aside something else that does need to be managed or processed at some point. And of course, sometimes despite our best efforts we can't keep something from having an effect then and there.

EXAMPLE

Jim and the Dice

For example, last time while Jim was playing a board game with his family, the dice hitting the board took him out of the moment.

It reminded him of the mass casualty shooting, where when he put the girl on the stretcher, a plastic toy fell out of her hand and hit the ground. The sound of the dice hitting the board suddenly reminded him of that moment.

While not quite a full flashback, the shift in his mood about that moment shows that there's still something about that experience that bothers him.

NOTES

....
....
....
....
....
....
....
....
....
....

Noticing When Something Needs Attention

It's important to know how to recognize the signs. That way, you can make a plan to work through things. In this part, we'll look at:

- Your role as the 'Compartment Supervisor'
- The signs and symptoms of compartment overflow
- Overflow examples and tips

Let's start with the important role you have here.

You as the **Compartment Supervisor**.

The thing about all the compartments and different areas of your life is that they **don't manage themselves**. If someone doesn't look after them, they can cause all kinds of trouble. Here are some examples:

- Spending more than you earn and racking up lots of debt can cause financial difficulties
- Maintaining a healthy relationship with a partner takes ongoing investment
- Avoiding exercise and eating lots of unhealthy foods can cause health issues down the track

Naturally, you are in charge of all the different areas of your life. In terms of compartmenting, it means that you are the **Compartment Supervisor** that keeps an eye on everything that's happening.

COMPARTMENT SUPERVISOR — YOU KEEP AN EYE ON THINGS TO SEE WHAT'S HAPPENING OVERALL & WATCH FOR OVERFLOW

Of course, this seems entirely obvious, though the **self-awareness** to be developed through this is not quite as simple.

Self-awareness here means being able to detect how something in one compartment is affecting others.

EXAMPLE

Jim and the Dice – Alternate Universe

Let's imagine that our friend Jim wasn't quite as good with self-awareness while playing the board game with his family. Maybe it would have gone something like this:

- They're playing the game and everyone's having fun
- The sound of the dice hitting the board unexpectedly brings back emotions from work for Jim
- Jim doesn't understand what is making him feel this way, so he goes quiet and withdraws
- His wife notices and asks what's wrong. *"Nothing, just keep playing,"* says Jim. *"Obviously something's wrong,"* replied his wife. Jim raises his voice *"It's nothing! I just don't feel like playing this stupid game!"* shoving the game to the side, knocking things over
- His child starts crying and he ends up having a big fight with his wife about unrelated things

This type of escalation happens easily, and it can cause all kinds of unnecessary damage to relationships as well as result in destructive behavior (drinking, etc.).

To avoid this, you need a clear view about what's happening in your own mind, and the self-awareness to recognize when something in one area might be affecting you in other areas.

One way to increase self-awareness is to be able to recognize the signs of what we call overflow.

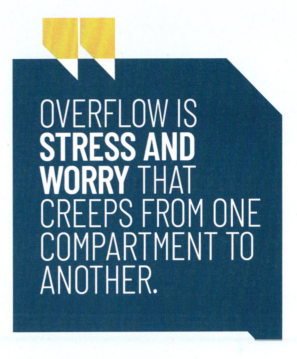

OVERFLOW IS **STRESS AND WORRY** THAT CREEPS FROM ONE COMPARTMENT TO ANOTHER.

The Signs of Overflow

Overflow is stress and worry that creeps from one compartment to another.

This effectively means that something isn't properly compartmented, so you can't be fully present in the moment you are in.

Here we are mainly looking at signs that you are being affected in some way that is not appropriate for the situation you are in. For example, Jim getting angry during the board game was clearly not caused by the game itself or his family, but rather something that he previously experienced at work.

COMPARTMENT **OVERFLOW**

EXAMPLE - CONFLICT WITH FAMILY IS AFFECTING THE HOBBIES, PARTNER AND ME BOXES.

ACTIVITY 4.1.5

Thinking about these signs of overflow, do you notice some of these yourself?

◢ ....

◢ ....

◢ ....

◢ ....

◢ ....

◢ ....

◢ ....

◢ ....

◢ ....

How can compartmenting help with the signs you've experienced?

◢ ....

◢ ....

◢ ....

◢ ....

◢ ....

◢ ....

◢ ....

◢ ....

◢ ....

◢ ....

◢ ....

Symptoms of compartment overflow include the following:

◢ Being distracted and preoccupied

◢ Unable to relax

◢ Easily angered over small things

◢ Feeling tense and unsure why

◢ Feeling exhausted

◢ Irritability for no clear reason

◢ Struggling to focus and concentrate

◢ Unexplained headaches

◢ Difficulty sleeping

◢ Upset stomach & digestion problems

The overarching theme here is that in some way you are unable to be fully present where you want to be. For example, you struggle to enjoy a hobby because of something that happened with your family earlier that day.

The goal then is to improve your compartmenting ability so that you can be present with what you are doing, and then manage challenges in other areas when appropriate. This means:

◢ Detecting overflow

◢ Managing overflow

◢ And improving your mental skills to be able to prevent overflow in future

Another tell-tale sign of potential overflow is when peeking into a compartment causes it to **burst open uncontrollably**. For example, if someone asks about work and you **instantly get stressed or irritated**, then there might be something to explore.

Sometimes you might not even notice it yourself, but someone close might mention that bringing up some topics with you is like opening a high-pressure gas tank.

WATCH FOR **SENSITIVE SUBJECTS**

IF BRINGING UP A SUBJECT LEADS TO EMOTIONAL OUTBURSTS, THEN IT SHOULD BE EXPLORED.

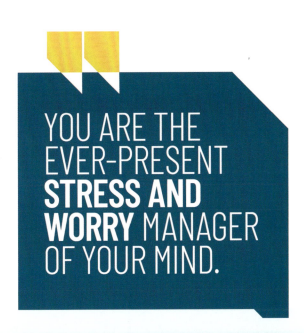

4.1.4 Compartment Communication

Compartmenting helps you stay present and focused in the moment wherever you are. Developing your skills here can eventually help you manage and avoid overflow by working through challenges without unnecessary delays.

Though, what happens in the meantime? Are you supposed to be quiet about the things you are going through and deal with stuff in silence?

Most definitely not! **Sustainable compartmenting is a tool that enables you to communicate about these challenges more effectively**. Let's see how this works.

Different Communication Styles

Let's think back to our friend Jim. In one scenario he was unable to communicate properly and ended up causing a big fight with his family. In the other scenario, he quickly became aware of what was happening in his mind and could communicate effectively.

There, compartmenting helped make a difference, though the part that made the biggest difference was his role as the Compartment Supervisor.

As the Compartment Supervisor, you are the ever-present manager of your mind. This role is therefore not only important to identify problems and start working on solutions, but also to be able to **communicate what's happening** to other people (just like a real supervisor would report issues).

To visualize this, you can literally think of it as the following picture where you are above all these boxes looking down and keeping an eye on a problem down below.

You can then write on top of the box that there's something to deal with. The advantage here is that you can tell someone about a problem somewhere in your life without actually having to open that box and feel those emotions right in that moment.

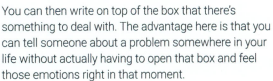

NOTES

....
....
....
....
....
....
....
....
....
....
....
....
....
....
....
....
....
....
....
....
....
....
....
....

EXAMPLE

Jim's Conversation – Analysis

When Jim was playing the board game with his family, he was able to quickly identify that something in the work box was about to overflow to the family box.

Through using the **catch and pause** technique, he managed to prevent that overflow so he could stay present with his family and enjoy that time.

What he said at that time was:

"Hmm… was just thinking about something that happened at work"

Here he had the presence of mind to acknowledge the moment, especially since the people around him noticed it too. This is important to reduce concern in others (letting them know that you are aware of what they noticed).

Then he says to his wife:

"I'll tell you about it later"

This is also important because he's letting his partner know that he won't keep her in the dark about what he's dealing with. He also sets the expectation of when they will talk about it, helping to reduce worry for her, and lets her know that he trusts her enough to be open with her.

Then later that night once their child is off to bed, Jim and his wife are in the bedroom, and he finally tells her what happened.

At this point it's likely he'll break down and cry, fully experiencing the emotions built up from that experience that he hasn't really worked through yet. Talking through the experience starts to separate the emotion from the memory, helping to process what happened.

The Difference

An advantage here is that they are both prepared for this moment. And as difficult as it is, the **conversation builds trust and understanding** between them while helping to process the experience. At the same time, their child is tucked away, and Jim doesn't need to worry about having to explain the harsh realities of life to a young and innocent mind just yet.

Compare this to the Alternate Universe example where Jim didn't have compartmenting in place. There he had an outburst that scared his son and caused a fight with his wife.

This is how something as simple as a pair of dice can result in either a destructive moment, **or a constructive moment that strengthens a family**.

Here it's helpful to have partners also do this training so you can both understand the strategies used to help strengthen the relationship.

EXAMPLE

Jim's Conversation – Emery

The same style of conversation can be applied to all kinds of situations. The result being the ability to talk about difficult challenges you are working through with anyone without having to break down with anyone right there and then.

For example, Jim runs into a colleague that he doesn't know that well but sees every few days or so.

Emery (the colleague): *"Hey Jim, how've you been?"*

Jim: *"Yeah good, you?"*

Emery: *"Pretty good! So, all good with you these days?"*

Jim: *"Ah yeah... pretty much"*

Emery: *"...really? You seem to have been a bit quiet lately."* – Seems that Emery is interested in more than exchanging the usual pleasantries, inviting Jim to open up more.

Jim: *"Noticed, hey? Well... there was something from a while back that's been on my mind lately. You know how this job is."* – Jim can again acknowledge what's been happening, though it's not quite the time to open up about all the details just yet.

Emery: *"Yeah, I know... Want to talk about it?"*

Jim: *"I'm ok so far. I've been talking to my wife about all this stuff and she's been great. Though if that doesn't work, I'll let you know!"* – Seems Jim doesn't know Emery well enough to want to open up about everything just yet.

Perhaps he prefers to talk with colleagues that he's closer with, though he leaves the door open to chat with Emery if needed later.

Emery: *"Glad you're talking to someone about this stuff. Helps me to get that stuff out too. Let's catch up some time anyway hey?"*

Jim: *"Sounds good, later!"*

This example shows how compartmenting can help you communicate more honestly about what's happening in your mind and also give people confidence that you are actively working through those challenges. Even with people you don't know that well, you can still be honest about your life and not have to worry as much about feeling all those emotions in the moment.

More Communication Strategies

Another thing to consider is how to share which compartments and when. This can be more important when you deal with things that can be tough for others. Some examples of when this could be useful are:

- **Limiting time** – For example, when there is lots of conflict within your extended family, it could become a frequent topic to complain about the latest incident. This could become overwhelming, so there might be an agreement to keep the family box closed at least over dinner and save those for another occasion

- **Sharing broadly** – If you work daily with something that might be disturbing to others, it could be tough for them to hear about it every day if they don't have the same mental toughness as you. Here you might agree to share more broadly what happened without going into too much detail

- **Using euphemisms** – Sometimes with colleagues you may use specific words in that compartment to be more factual and accurate. Examples are terms like 'expired', 'terminal', or 'cadaver'. These terms are less emotional and make it mentally easier when regularly handling these situations

Little changes like these can help maintain a good balance so you can talk about what's happening with less emotional load on yourself and others.

Though, not all situations are easy to simply work through. Here we can look at how to escalate self-care as needed for the situation.

ACTIVITY 4.1.6

Do you have some approach like stepped self-care?

....

....

....

....

....

....

....

....

....

....

How do you manage tough challenges?

....

....

....

....

....

....

....

....

....

....

....

....

4.1.5   Stepped Self-Care

You can take a stepped approach when you've experienced a tough situation at work or if there's something that's bothering you elsewhere in life. Of course, there's no set way for how everyone should deal with things, so take the steps below as a general strategy that you can adopt to your own style and to the specific event.

1. **Talk early on –** Soon after a difficult experience (preferably on the same day), it can help to just mention it to someone. This doesn't need to be a big conversation, but rather just acknowledging it, like *"Wow, that was crazy"*, or *"Today was rough"*. Something as simple as that can already start to help process things and confirm that it was something out of the ordinary and share that load with someone else. You can also tell me about it by checking in with the emojis on the home page

2. **Sleep on it –** Many challenges you'll face will be temporary events that feel tough during the first day, and then after some good sleep you're already moving on. The next day, check in with yourself and see how you feel. If you're doing fine, then you can move on. Otherwise, if it's still bothering you, then move to the next step

3. **Think through it –** At this step set some time aside for yourself to think through the experience in more detail. You can do this by yourself and let yourself feel whatever emotions come up. You can try this for a few days to about a week and see if you start to feel better as you go through

4. **Talk in detail –** If you feel like you're struggling to move on, then it can help to have deeper discussions with others. Could be a partner, colleagues, family, friends, etc. Sharing pain is a good way to lessen it. Of course, you can do this earlier as well if you like. If you start to feel better here in about two weeks, then you're heading in the right direction. It might still take longer to get back to your usual self, but that's just part of the process

5. **Get structured help –** Otherwise if after two weeks you feel the same or even worse than at the start, then it's likely time to reach out for more structured and professional help. This can be through your organization, helplines, or arranged by yourself. Find out what's available to you and use it. It's better to work through these things early than to avoid that box in the corner of your mind for months or years

As before, you don't have to follow this exact plan, though it is a useful guide to track progress. As a visualisation technique, you can label the box affected by this to mark where you're up to with the escalation steps above. That way you can keep track and be honest with yourself about how you're dealing with what happened.

Compartmenting is a broad strategy that helps you organize and discipline your mind. It also enables you to understand what's happening in your mind and communicate that with others more effectively.

Practice this as a tool to sustain your effectiveness and high performance throughout your career.

SCAN ME

Sustainable Compartmenting
in the **Driven Resilience App**

Scan the link to access the skill in the app (make sure you are **logged into the app** first).

app.hellodriven.com/activities/1232

NOTES

REASONING

4.2

OPTIMIZING
THOUGHTS &
BEHAVIORS

4.2 OPTIMIZING THOUGHTS & BEHAVIORS

Learing Outcomes:

- Understand the basics of triggers, beliefs and behaviors
- Understand the value of challenging beliefs to change behaviors
- Learn about 10 thought distortions, how to identify them, and potential actions to improve

This is Useful For:

- Identifying ways in which default thinking is affecting daily life
- Developing more accurate and helpful thinking patterns

To help understand what it is, consider this - do If you think about your brain in a very simplified way, it works like this:

1. An event that triggers a neural response
2. The brain processes that event based on your beliefs
3. A behavior or thought is produced

The things you do aren't automatic. **Your behaviors, thoughts, and emotions come from what you believe.**

For example, if you believe it is embarrassing to show up late for an appointment, then you'd probably get anxious if you get delayed in traffic. That is a natural response based on your belief. Is that an appropriate belief? That's the more relevant question.

4.2.1 About Thoughts & Behaviors

By understanding this basic process of how your mind leads you to think or behave in certain ways, you can then consider if a particular belief is useful.

This is the basis of **Cognitive Behavioral Therapy (CBT)**, which is one of the most successful therapies used to overcome depression, anxiety, and many other mental health issues. CBT represents this interaction between thoughts, feelings, and behaviors, which revolve around beliefs.

This is not only useful for treating mental illness, but also for everyone to build a more disciplined mind. Learning the techniques used in CBT can also help to protect your mind and help build resilience. This not only benefits you, but also those you work with in the field.

Noticing Unhelpful Behaviors

What is challenging with beliefs is that they tend to hide away. Asking yourself *"What are my beliefs?"* will likely draw a blank in your mind. So, let's try this...

ACTIVITY 4.2.1

Vanilla ice cream is the best flavor in the world!

What is your response to this statement? Do you agree, or perhaps you instantly feel that is totally incorrect since it's basically the most boring flavor of them all?

....

....

....

....

Here you experienced the exploration of a belief, with the process being:

1. **The trigger –** Hearing about someone's love for vanilla ice cream
2. **Your belief –** Vanilla is not the best ice cream
3. **Your behavior –** A feeling of disbelief and saying what you think of that statement

This is why it's important to look for behaviors, since they give you clues about what your beliefs are. Just like with the ice cream example, it can feel like the statement about it being a boring flavor comes automatically, but right after you say it, you can then reflect: *"Why did I say that? I guess I believe vanilla is a boring flavor!"*

Reflect on your belief and behavior that follows from that statement. What was your belief? And what was the behavior that followed?

....

....

....

....

....

....

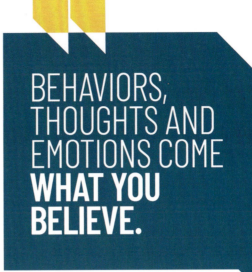

BEHAVIORS, THOUGHTS AND EMOTIONS COME WHAT YOU BELIEVE.

The key is, having a belief, and **knowing that you have that specific belief** are two totally different things. Knowing your own beliefs is a whole new level of self-awareness that comes with a lot of personal power. With that knowledge comes the ability to challenge and change beliefs that are no longer helpful.

Why Change Beliefs?

That's a good question that might be on your mind (perhaps you have a belief that beliefs are not important?) For your taste in ice cream, the impact of the belief is small. However, beliefs quickly scale into much bigger parts of life that can have a huge impact on your mental wellbeing.

For example, if a paramedic believes losing a patient on a call is a personal failure and is their own fault, it might look like this:

1. **Trigger –** Losing a patient
2. **Belief –** I should never lose patients
3. **Behavior –** Thought: *"I am worthless"* Emotion: Shame, guilt

This is a major challenge, since the problem with emotions like guilt and shame is that they wear people down mentally. This adds up over time, and contributes to anxiety, depression, and other mental health issues.

Challenging this belief can allow you to upgrade it, for example:

1. **Trigger –** Losing a patient
2. **Belief –** Not everyone can be saved, but I will always do my best
3. **Behavior –** Thought: *"That was unfortunate"* Emotion: Sadness, yet determined and hopeful for the next patient

Explore and Upgrade

We talk about 'upgrading' beliefs since that is what generally happens in the brain. When you change an unhelpful belief to a more constructive one, you tend to feel less stressed, more confident, and more motivated. It's literally like you are upgrading your brain.

To explore more places where you might have beliefs that could be challenged, let's work through a set of thought distortions so you can check if you recognize any.

 **ACTIVITY 4.2.2**

10 Thought Distortions

In the remainder of this section, we'll explore ten different thought distortions. We all have some of these, and these distortions affect your perspectives and experience of life daily.

These thought distortions are ways in which your thinking might be **biased**, so the hardest part is often recognizing that you might think this way.

Though once you recognize it, then you can start to upgrade towards more accurate ways of thinking – you can start to get more clarity and see the world through a realistic lens.

With each of these, **tick the box** if you have noticed it in your own behavior, and write down your experience.

4.2.2 Shoulds

Have you ever felt that you're not living up to expectations of yourself?

For example: *"I **should** not make mistakes"* or *"I **should** have done that better"*, and annoyed when it's not the case...

Or you felt frustrated that other people are not living up to your expectations?

For example: *"He **should** have known better"* or *"She **shouldn't** have done that"*

This thought distortion is called **'overgeneralization'**. This is where you make broad, usually negative, statements about yourself or others. Often this is based on a single event that isn't nearly enough evidence to make such a broad judgement.

Using words like **always, never, ever, or all**, can be signs that you're overgeneralizing. It's important to separate fact from opinion in these instances and try not to use words like 'always' and 'never' when thinking of yourself or other people.

Usually, it's best to avoid using these words overall. Situations change, people change and learn. Don't close your mind unnecessarily by thinking in absolutes.

Yes, I've noticed this.

What has your experience with this so far?

....
....
....
....
....
....
....
....
....
....

NOTES

....
....
....
....
....
....
....
....
....
....
....
....
....
....

4.2.3 Overgeneralization

Do you ever find yourself thinking:

- *"I always mess up"*
- *Seeing someone struggling with a task and thinking "He'll never make it"*
- *"She never gets things right"*
- *"I always do that"*
- *Perhaps you went on a bad date and thought "I'll never find love..."*
- *Or see something terrible and think "All people are evil"*

This thought distortion is called '**shoulds**' and it shows up as unreasonably high expectations and rules we have for ourselves, usually resulting in shame or guilt. Or we might hold others to an unreasonably high standard, and the 'shoulds' can result in anger and frustration.

While not all 'shoulds' are bad, it's important to recognize when they negatively impact our behavior towards ourselves or others.

A simple way to challenge this is to ask yourself:

- *"Are these expectations necessary?"*
- *"How would life be different if I relaxed these standards?"*
- If certain expectations or standards are necessary, what actions can you take proactively to help people meet those, or allow yourself to live up to them? For example, training, regular check-ins, etc.

Yes, I've noticed this.

What has your experience with this so far?

....
....
....
....
....
....
....
....
....
....

NOTES

....
....
....
....
....
....
....
....
....
....
....
....

4.2.4 Jumping to Conclusions

Do you tend to make predictions about the future? For example:

- You see people laughing and think that they must be laughing at you
- Or maybe you assume someone is angry at you without actually asking them
- Or you assume you won't get a promotion, so you don't even bother applying

These are examples of '**jumping to conclusions**'. Here you tend to make a prediction about how something might turn out, or how someone feels about you without finding evidence. As much as we feel that these assumptions may be true, it's important to explore the hard evidence behind these negative conclusions. Often you will find the reality is very different.

You could consider two approaches:

- **If it's something important** (like thinking you're probably not suited for a task you really want to work on), then instead ask people and gather evidence. You'll likely find some positive news
- **If it's something unimportant**, or alternatively something that you wouldn't find out about anyway (like wondering if two people whispering were talking about you), then it's much simpler to let it go and just assume it's likely something else. After all, speculating on unimportant events is generally not worth the energy

With other people, form your opinions on repeated behavior, and go out of your way to find out if there is evidence that opposes your view.

Yes, I've noticed this.

What has your experience with this so far?

....
....
....
....
....
....
....
....
....

NOTES

....
....
....
....
....
....
....
....
....
....
....

4.2.5 Personalization

Do you ever blame yourself for things that you have little control over, or often feel like things people do or say are because of you?

For instance, you might blame yourself for your neighbor's dog getting injured because you weren't home to notice the gate was open.

Or maybe you're at a party and see your friend looking unhappy, and you blame yourself for not spending enough time with them, even though she was in reality having a great time and was just in deep thought for a moment.

This distortion is called '**personalization**'. This is where you blame yourself for things that are out of your control, but totally believe that it was your fault. This often means you take things very personally, feeling like everything is aimed at you, or was your fault.

It can affect your self-esteem and generate negative emotions towards yourself, even though you did your best, or were not to blame, not the cause, or what people did wasn't aimed at you at all.

Challenge yourself to be realistic about how much control you truly had. Ask friends what they think and get some external perspectives.

Yes, I've noticed this.

What has your experience with this so far?

....

....

....

....

....

....

....

....

....

....

NOTES

....

....

....

....

....

....

....

....

....

....

....

....

....

4.2.6 'Just World' Fallacy

Do you tend to feel disappointed if a good deed goes unrewarded?

Alternatively, do you feel frustration or resentment towards someone when their bad deeds go unpunished?

You could have worked really hard for a promotion that a colleague got instead, so you feel that they were undeserving and get angry at them.

This distortion is called **'just world' fallacy'**, which is characterized by the thought that good deeds have to be rewarded, and bad deeds have to be punished. Although living in a fair world would be ideal, we have to remember that some events are out of the control of what's fair and just, and in reality, bad things can happen to good people, and good things can happen to people who don't necessarily deserve it.

The reality is that the only fairness in the world is that which we fight for ourselves. While the world may not be fair overall, we can aim to treat people fairly ourselves and create a fairer world for the people around us.

Yes, I've noticed this.

What has your experience with this so far?

....

....

....

....

....

....

....

....

....

NOTES

....

....

....

....

....

....

....

....

....

....

....

....

4.2.7 Black & White Thinking

Do you ever find yourself thinking along these lines?

Here are some examples:

- *"If I'm not winning, I'm losing"*
- *"You're either with me or against me"*
- *"If this person doesn't want to date me, then I'm never talking to them again"*
- *"If I don't pass this test, then I'll quit"*
- *"Everybody hates me"*
- *"There's a right way and a wrong way"*

For example, a student could get 97% on an exam but think they are a failure because they didn't get 100%. The student is unhappy with the result, even though it's an outstanding result.

This distortion is called '**black and white thinking**'. It's where you often see the absolutes (black or white) of a situation and find it hard to see shades of grey. Most of life is in the grey areas – situations that are not quite as we want them to be, but still pretty good given the right perspective.

Sometimes black and white thinking can even lead to self-fulfilling prophecies. Such as giving up on dating due to one bad date, which of course means much less chance of meeting a new romantic partner.

It's important to remember that everyone wins some and loses some. There are a lot of opportunities that come from being comfortable in living in the shades of grey.

Here are some ideas to challenge this thinking:

- Ask yourself if there really is no middle ground
- And what would it mean if there was a middle ground?
- Ask other people – do they see other ways in which things could be?

Yes, I've noticed this.

What has your experience with this so far?

....

....

....

....

....

....

....

....

....

NOTES

....

....

....

....

....

....

....

....

....

....

....

....

4.2.8 Global Labeling

Do you sometimes label yourself or someone else negatively, based on only one or two experiences? For example:

- ◢ This could be telling yourself *"I'm not good enough"*
- ◢ Labelling someone *"an idiot"* after only doing something wrong once
- ◢ Maybe after making one mistake, you say to yourself *"I'm useless"*

These are examples of '**global labeling**', which is when we create extreme and often negative statements about ourselves, or others based on very few experiences.

These could be based on a small mistake that anyone might make and are valuable learning experiences to improve yourself in the future.

It's helpful to keep in mind that **negative labels generally don't work well**. Both labels for yourself, and labels for other people. Just because you failed at something doesn't mean you're a failure. It just means that particular attempt didn't work - now it's time to try again until you succeed. Keep that in mind for other people as well. Success comes by learning from repeated failures – this is resilience.

☐ **Yes, I've noticed this.**

What has your experience with this so far?

◢ ....

◢ ....

◢ ....

◢ ....

◢ ....

◢ ....

◢ ....

◢ ....

◢ ....

◢ ....

NOTES

◢ ....

◢ ....

◢ ....

◢ ....

◢ ....

◢ ....

◢ ....

◢ ....

◢ ....

◢ ....

◢ ....

◢ ....

◢ ....

4.2.9 Control Fallacies

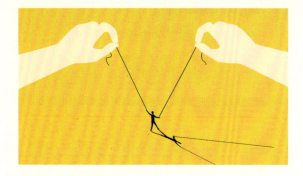

Have you ever felt that everything that happens to you is fate and that you have no control over it?

Or maybe, have you felt that you have complete control over your life and are also solely responsible for the lives of those around you?

For the first thought, an example could be saying something like *"my job really sucks and there's nothing I can do about it"*, even though you could always look for another job.

An example for the second thought could be feeling responsible that your friends didn't enjoy the movie you went to see, even though they are responsible for their own choices and the consequences.

This distortion is called '**control fallacies**'. They are when you take either full blame or no blame for the events in your life, even though the reality is always more in the middle, where we have some control, but not full control.

The aim here is to get a more **realistic appraisal** of different situations, so take a step back and consider:

- How much control do you really have? Sometimes you have less control than you think, sometimes you have more!
- Also, how much control should you have? If you're trying to control someone else's life, often it's better to take a step back and let them be their own person

When you really start to question yourself like this and explore your beliefs, you can move away from the extremes.

This will help you have more realistic expectations, reducing frustration, reducing anger, reducing anxiety.

☐ **Yes, I've noticed this.**

What has your experience with this so far?

....

....

....

....

....

....

....

....

....

....

NOTES

....

....

....

....

....

....

....

....

....

....

....

....

4.2.10 Mental Filtering

Do you tend to:

- Discount or ignore positive things that happen. Whether it's a compliment or a positive event, maybe you feel that you didn't deserve it, or it's not that good anyway
- For example, someone compliments you and you think *"she only said it to be nice"*
- Or maybe many people say happy birthday to you, except for one person. Then you spend all day wondering about that one person...
- It could feel like one bad thing ruins the whole day

This distortion is called '**mental filtering**'.

Having this thought distortion can drain the excitement out of your life and can often leave you feeling miserable, even though there is so much positivity that you can experience.

If something positive happens, try simply to accept it at face value and enjoy the feeling. You can still plan for potential negatives, but planning for what might go wrong shouldn't mean you forget to enjoy the potential upside.

One way to challenge mental filtering is to deliberately focus on appreciating the good moments. This helps people enjoy life more and is covered in the **Three Good Things** skill in Tenacity.

Another way to challenge this is reappraising the hard moments in life, helping you take experiences in your stride. This is covered in the **Reappraisal** skill as part of Composure.

Yes, I've noticed this.

What has your experience with this so far?

NOTES

4.2.11 Catastrophizing

Do you sometimes find yourself exaggerating a situation, or believing the worst-case scenario may happen and blowing up small situations until it feels like a major catastrophe is coming? For example, do you:

▲ Always expect the worst-case scenario?

▲ Blow up any small situation to feel like a disaster?

▲ Such as sending an email with a mistake and feeling like you'll lose your job?

▲ Or making a small mistake and it consumes you for the rest of the day?

▲ Statements like *"If my relationship breaks up, I'll never love anyone else again"*, or *"If I lose my job, I lose everything"*?

☐ **Yes, I've noticed this.**

What has your experience with this so far?

....
....
....
....
....
....
....
....
....
....
....
....

This is a very common distortion called '**catastrophizing**'. This is when we tend to make the worst out of any situation, and we worry far more than we need to.

When we mentally escalate situations, it can lead to severe imagined outcomes.

EXAMPLE

Bad Day at Work

For example, someone who is struggling with work might worry about being fired and unable to find a new job, and their partner then wanting a divorce, and them losing everything in the divorce so there will be nothing left anyway... So, what's the point of even trying, or even living at all? At that point, this person might even start to think about suicide.

Meanwhile, nothing here has actually happened and in reality, it's just a bad day at work.

This example shows just how extreme the consequences of a thought distortion like this can be. It highlights how closely you should monitor yourself for this type of thinking and look for signs of this from the people around you.

If you notice yourself catastrophizing, think about this:

- What's the **worst-case** scenario?
- What's the **best-case** scenario?
- What's the **most likely** scenario?

Usually, you'd find the most likely scenario tends to be close to the best-case scenario. For example, parents not being able to get in touch with their child and fearing the child is lying in a ditch somewhere - meanwhile the child's phone ran out of battery and they're on their way home already.

People often don't realize they are catastrophizing. It's like a thinking spiral that just keeps going from one terrible scenario to the next, never quite stopping to notice the thought patterns.

Noticing which of these thought distortions affect you can be difficult. Mainly since they tend to sit in blind spots. After all, you rarely feel that how you think is wrong. Since if you did, then you'd change it, right?

Here it's helpful to talk to other people. Ask them if they notice you sometimes thinking in unhelpful ways. People who are close to you are likely to recognize these things. So, ask them and be open to what they have to say. You might learn some interesting things about your own beliefs.

TECHNIQUE

14-Day Rewire Program

Exploring thought distortions can be a challenging process. When you find ones here that are making life significantly harder than it needs to be, it can be helpful to work with a therapist or counselor to work through them and build a more useful belief system.

Alternatively, in the Driven Resilience App there is a 14-day program called Rewire, which uses Cognitive Behavioral strategies to work through these distortions, explore them in more detail, and build new beliefs in the process.

You can start this course any time as long as you have an active subscription to the Driven Resilience App. Simply scan the code below to access the Rewire program and start:

PS – make sure you are logged into your app to access this technique.

app.hellodriven.com/activities/511

Optimizing Thoughts & Behaviors in the Driven Resilience App

Scan the link to access the skill in the app (make sure you are **logged into the app** first).

app.hellodriven.com/activities/1233

NOTES

REASONING

4.3

CONCRETE VS ABSTRACT PROCESSING

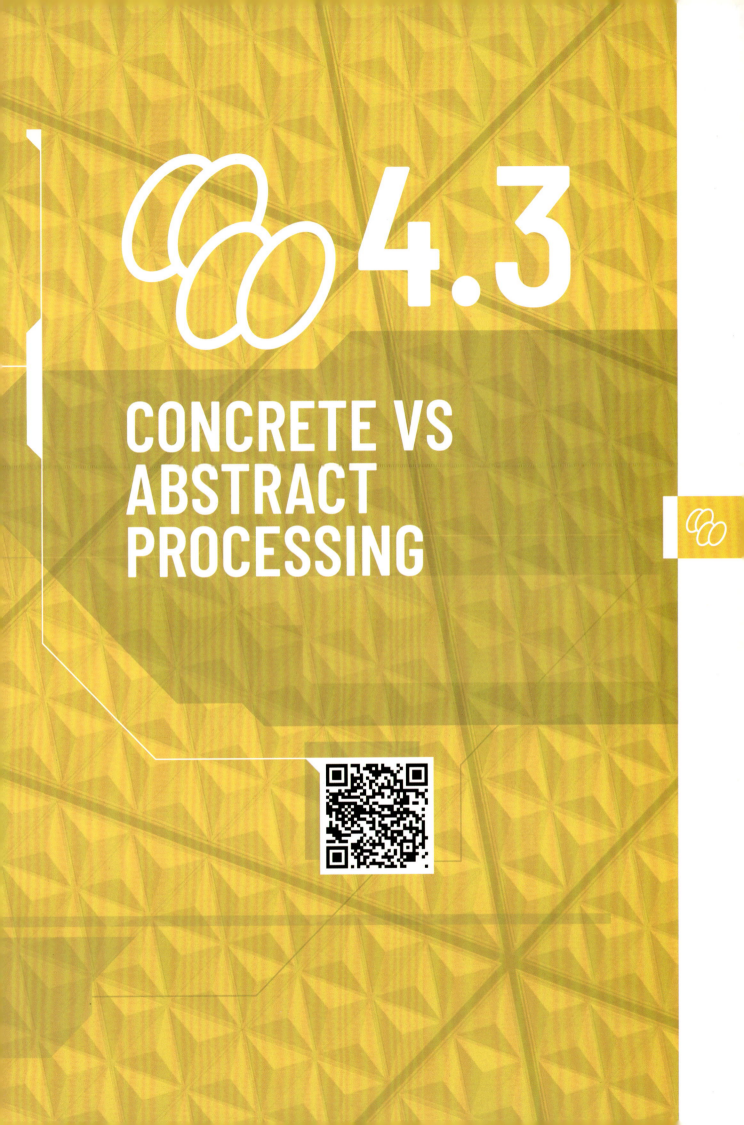

4.3 CONCRETE VS ABSTRACT PROCESSING

Learing Outcomes:

- Understand the differences between the types of processing styles
- Understand the pitfalls of abstract processing
- Learn and practice the concrete processing technique

This is Useful For:

- Reduce the mental impact of difficult situations

The reality for many first responders, military personnel and others is that over time, exposure to difficult events can contribute to burnout and PTSI. Therefore, using a technique to effectively process these events is important for your ongoing resilience, wellbeing, and sustainable performance.

Two Processing Methods

Let's consider two ways in which people tend to process difficult events:

- Abstract processing – which includes thought traps that can make things worse
- Concrete processing – which leads to better outcomes

Quite simply this means we want to use concrete processing when facing difficult situations. To understand this better, let's explore abstract processing first.

4.3.1 Abstract Processing

Abstract processing comes from a natural human tendency to try and make sense of events. This includes asking questions like:

- *"Why do bad things happen to good people?"*
- *"Why is the world so messed up?"*
- *"Why do accidents have to happen?"*
- *"Why do people have to suffer like this?"*
- *"What does this mean?"*
- *"Why can't I just fix this?"*

It's in our nature to ask these questions to try and make sense of the world. Though there's one big problem – **these questions are unanswerable**. That means there's no clear way to resolve them and move on.

QUICK TEST

Concrete Processing Skill Check

Scan the code below to complete a short assessment of your current approach with concrete vs abstract processing. You can do this assessment again later to see how your skill changes over time.

PS – make sure you are logged into your app to access this assessment.

app.hellodriven.com/activities/793

These questions lead to **rumination**, which is when you keep thinking about something without any resolution or action. Research shows us that focusing on these questions leads to problems:

- It can increase intrusive memories and flashbacks
- It leads to a higher likelihood of PTSI symptoms
- It reduces problem-solving skills
- It can increase feelings of anxiety and reduce the ability to cope

The reason for this lies in the brain, as the event sticks out in your mind – **it doesn't fit** with everything else you know. This increases limbic brain activation, causing the problems listed above.

What's needed is for there to be a clear and cohesive story to properly make sense of the event.

ACTIVITY 4.3.1

Do you sometimes find yourself asking these questions in your work?

....
....
....
....
....
....
....
....
....
....

What kind of situations make you ask these types of questions?

....
....
....
....
....
....
....

4.3.2 Concrete Processing

It's here that concrete processing shows a better way to think about difficult events. Concrete processing focuses on the exact details, asking questions that can be answered fully through investigation.

Questions include:

- ◢ *"What exactly happened?"*
- ◢ *"Who was involved in this event?"*
- ◢ *"How exactly did this happen?"*
- ◢ *"What were the events that lead to this outcome?"*
- ◢ *"What practical steps could have been taken to prevent this from happening?"*
- ◢ *"What do I now do with this information?"*

Here you can see, each question has a factual, concrete answer. The benefit here is that in your mind, concrete processing creates a **logical narrative – a story that makes sense**.

This logical story lets the limbic brain know that this isn't something strange, it's not something to fear. Therefore, you disconnect the memory of the event from the emotions. This helps you to remember difficult events without causing mental pain.

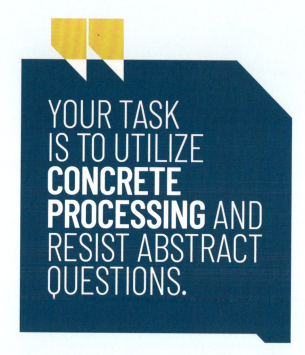

YOUR TASK IS TO UTILIZE **CONCRETE PROCESSING** AND RESIST ABSTRACT QUESTIONS.

Using this method shows positive results[4]:

- ◢ Reduced emotional processing and more logical processing
- ◢ Fewer intrusive memories and flashbacks
- ◢ Reduced symptoms of PTSI
- ◢ Reduced feelings of anxiety
- ◢ Increased problem-solving skills (you're able to fully activate the prefrontal cortex)

There are lots of benefits to using this approach. Your task is to utilize concrete processing and resist abstract questions.

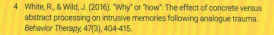

4   White, R., & Wild, J. (2016). "Why" or "how": The effect of concrete versus abstract processing on intrusive memories following analogue trauma. *Behavior Therapy*, 47(3), 404-415.

Concrete Processing Technique

1. Focus on **specific** and **objective** details
2. In your mind, form a **logical timeline** of events
3. Set out what **specific steps** need to happen from here

This is a technique that has been proven to work - so using this as a regular form of mental discipline can make you more effective in your work. It helps you stay mentally healthy and sustain high performance.

Practicing this regularly helps to form a level of **professional detachment**, which is necessary in many high adversity occupations to be able to do your work in the long term without developing burnout or compassion fatigue.

You can also share this skill to help colleagues and team members focus on concrete details if you hear them asking abstract questions.

SCAN ME

TECHNIQUE

Concrete Processing

Use this step-by-step Concrete Processing technique to put the skill into action following a difficult event.

PS – make sure you are logged into your app to access this technique.

app.hellodriven.com/activities/1023

ACTIVITY 4.3.2

Practice Concrete Processing by exploring this scene you are tasked with responding to:

Focus on **specific** and **objective** details. What is a logical **timeline** of events here?

....
....
....
....
....
....

What **specific steps** need to be taken from here?

....
....
....
....
....
....
....

ACTIVITY 4.3.3

Practice Concrete Processing by exploring this scene you are tasked with responding to:

Focus on **specific** and **objective** details. What is a logical **timeline** of events here?

....
....
....
....
....
....

What **specific steps** need to be taken from here?

....
....
....
....
....
....
....
....

SCAN ME

Concrete vs Abstract Processing in the Driven Resilience App

Scan the link to access the skill in the app (make sure you are **logged into the app** first).

app.hellodriven.com/activities/1234

COMPOSURE

5.1

BRAIN-BALANCED BREATHING

5.1 BRAIN-BALANCED BREATHING

SKILL OVERVIEW

Learing Outcomes:

- Understand the fundamentals of brain activation states
- Learn how to apply breathing as a method to control brain activation
- Learn how to expand the technique using a grounding strategy

This is Useful For:

- Quickly regaining focus and mental clarity in high-stress situations
- Building awareness on when to apply this strategy

In high-pressure environments where every second counts, the ability to maintain calm and clear judgment can be the thin line between success and tragedy.

When you are at the forefront of critical incidents where the stakes are high, breathing techniques emerge as a vital tool that enables you to navigate the complex and demanding nature of the work with greater resilience and composure.

Indeed, the Composure domain is about **regulating emotions and managing stress**. To be able to do this, we need effective strategies to be able to quickly calm down limbic brain when we notice it activating too strongly.

Going back to the two key areas of the brain we explored before, here we can delve further into the effects of these areas and how we can manage them.

5.1.1   Breathing & Brain Activation

Previously we talked about activation of the **Limbic Brain** (LB), where we feel emotions like stress, being anxious, and many others that are often not 'enjoyable', so to speak.

On the other side we have activation of the **Prefrontal Cortex** (PFC), which is where we feel more open, engaged, and generally can focus better, solve problems, and be more accurate in our work.

From here we can map out different emotions. We see on the Limbic side we have **Displeasure** emotions, like grieving, while on the other side we have **Pleasure** emotions on the Frontal Cortex side, like feeling happy.

We also have emotions going from **Low Intensity** emotions, like feeling sleepy, to **High Intensity** emotions, like rage and ecstasy.

As a simplified way of thinking about these quadrants, we can classify them by the type of **neuro chemicals** that they are dominated by.

- The **red box** is fueled by adrenaline, generally activating the fight or flight response
- The **blue box** is fueled by cortisol, which can be longer lasting states that build up over time
- The **yellow box** is fueled by serotonin, which can also be longer lasting states that is generally helpful for our wellbeing
- The **green box** is fueled by dopamine, where we feel uplifting motivating emotions which can come and go quickly

Note – in reality, all neurochemicals are constantly active in some ways, so this illustration is more for the sake of simplicity to think about which neuro chemical tends to dominate that emotion.

All emotions are useful, since they give us an idea of how we currently best understand how to respond to what's happening in the environment. It's natural to shift between these emotions through the day, though when we find ourselves experiencing life more on the Limbic side, and further to the left of the Limbic side, then we can start to **experience negative impact on both our physical and mental health**.

This is where Composure comes in as a domain to help regulate and manage emotional activation, helping us shift to the right Frontal Cortex side, where we operate at our best.

ACTIVITY 5.1.1

Looking across that chart of emotions, which zone do you tend to experience in your work?

....

....

....

....

....

....

....

....

....

....

....

LIMBIC ACTIVATION

LIMBIC BRAIN (LB)

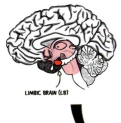

Adrenaline					**Dopamine**	
Terror	Rage	Distressed	Powerful	Elated	Ecstatic
Hate	Anxious	Tense	Astonished	Excited	Thrilled
Fear	Anger	Frustrated	Energetic	Cheerful	Joy
Defeat	Confused	Skeptical	Determined	Grateful	Happy
Grief	Annoyed	Worried	Thoughtful	Confident	Inspired

Displeasure — Intensity — Pleasure

Hurt	Jealous	Apprehensive	Engaged	Stimulated	Caring
Sad	Inferior	Cautious	Interested	Friendly	Hopeful
Miserable	Lonely	Distracted	Mellow	Peaceful	Content
Shame	Boredom	Tired	Calmness	Serene	Satisfied
Depressed	Bitter	Apathetic	Sleepy	Relieved	Relaxed

Cortisol   **Serotonin**

High / Low

FRONTAL ACTIVATION

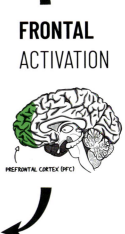

PREFRONTAL CORTEX (PFC)

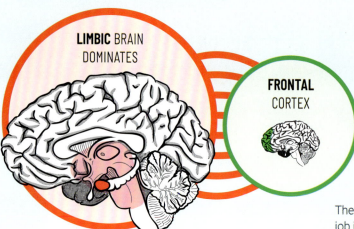

LIMBIC BRAIN
DOMINATES

FRONTAL
CORTEX

High Stress Imbalance

Often when dealing with high stress or high stakes situations, we get strong activation in the Limbic brain. When this happens, **blood flow to the frontal cortex is decreased** because the Limbic brain wants to prioritize fast and impulsive actions.

Unfortunately, this compromises good decision-making and reduces the accuracy of our work, because we need the Frontal Cortex to be able to deal with complex situations and make good strategic decisions.

This is why we need to **re-balance activation in the brain**, and we need to do it fast. Achieving a balance here is useful since **we want the clarity of the Frontal Cortex**, but also the energy that the Limbic brain provides.

In situations like this, we often can't take a few minutes to go for a walk and cool down. We need something that we can do in the moment, even while we are dealing with a situation.

Taking Control

This is where breathing comes in. We have a lot of automatic functions in the body, like how fast the heart beats, digestion, and many others. But only one of these can we consciously take over and decide to control directly, which is **breathing**.

Many people are familiar with breathing as a skill, but how exactly does it work?

This is through the interaction with a part of the brain called the **pre-Bötzinger complex**, or **PBC** for short, which communicates through the vagus nerve.

The PBC is located right above the brain stem, and its job is to communicate how fast you're breathing to the brain. When the fight-or-flight response activates, our breathing becomes faster to pump more oxygen into the body, getting it ready to respond. This would be great, if it didn't **reduce blood flow to the Frontal Cortex** at the same time!

As the rate of breathing increases, the PBC communicates this to the brain to tell it to focus on what's going on.

However, what's interesting and useful for us is that if we **consciously take control of our breathing and slow it down**, then the PBC communicates to the brain that it appears we are not in danger since we're not breathing quickly, effectively telling the limbic brain to calm down.

This way, you have a manual override switch to deactivate the limbic response through a breathing brake. **Slow your breathing, slow the limbic brain.**

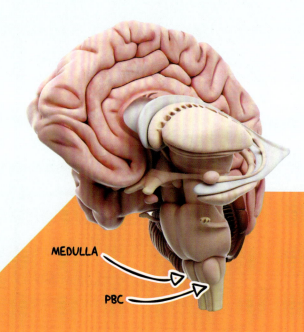

MEDULLA

PBC

5.1.2 Applying Brain-Balanced Breathing

The key point of this is that **we have an effective control strategy** in breathing that helps us deactivate the Limbic Brain.

To use the technique, you'll need to practice two steps:

Step 1 involves **recognizing the signs of stress**. This means being aware of what's physically happening to the body when it's stressed. This is often the hardest part, which is just about knowing when to use this technique. Especially since the times you need to use it, you might not be thinking clearly already. This is why practicing it at all kinds of different times is useful – you start to train yourself to recognize when you need it more and more, until it becomes more of a reflexive action. You can also ask a colleague to help you to identify when you can apply this to build your awareness.

Step 2 is **applying the technique** itself. The breathing method itself is a widely used technique called Box Breathing. This is a very simple and reliable way to control Limbic brain activation.

Limbic brain activation shows up all over the body. This is because the redirection of resources to get ready for fight or flight has some side effects. We explored these before in the Neuroscience section. Here's a reminder of the signs you might notice:

- Increased heart rate
- Fast and shallow breathing
- Tense muscles
- Sweating
- Flushed skin
- Shaking hands
- Difficulty speaking
- Dryness in the mouth

The key is that when you notice these, that is your sign to **balance brain activation with breathing**.

When you use your breathing brake, you slow down Limbic brain activation, and balance it so that the Frontal Cortex can activate.

The technique is simple – like we're moving along the sides of a box. Breathe in over the count of 4 seconds, hold for 4 seconds, breathe out for 4, and hold again for 4 before starting again. You can visualize the box as you do this.

ACTIVITY 5.1.2

Try Box Breathing:

 **Box Breathing**
4 seconds in, hold, out, hold

Doing this **reactivates the Prefrontal Cortex**, letting blood flow back to it so that it helps you regain composure and clarity in the moment. This helps you to then access the other domains of resilience, like Reasoning and Vision to help you be resourceful and solve problems strategically.

It's helpful to know that you don't need to do this technique exactly like this. The key is to slow down your breathing when you feel Limbic activation happen.

Almost instantly you'll slow down your heart rate, and your mind will start to become clearer. This is when it becomes useful in the moment when you don't have time to take a break and do box breathing in a technically correct way.

SCAN ME

 TECHNIQUE

Guided Calm Breathing

Scan the code below to use a step-by-step breathing technique with different modes in the Driven Resilience App – useful for when you need some guidance to relax LB activation.

PS – make sure you are logged into your app to access this technique.

app.hellodriven.com/activities/142

5.1.3 Rapid Regulation Through Grounding

Brain-Balanced Breathing provides the basic technique, though this can be enhanced by combining a concept called '**Grounding**'.

Strong activation of the limbic brain is an important sign to take charge again of your brain and bring you back into an effective state of mind.

Being able to **quickly regulate** limbic activation in this moment is particularly important when you face high-stress moments.

This gives you **clarity, increases accuracy,** and **results in better outcomes** for the people you look after.

Being able to adapt a strategy like breathing to be something you can use in your work and elsewhere makes it more useful, since you become better at applying it in the moment.

Grounding

Let's explore a way we can do this through Grounding.

This is a technique to **return focus to the present moment**, especially when the limbic brain activates and is trying to divert your attention elsewhere, like getting away (flight).

Grounding works through **activating the senses** – focusing on what you can see, touch, hear, smell, and taste.

Classically, a grounding exercise would involve a slow progression through these, but we often don't get that luxury of time to do this.

A rapid adaptation of this is to **take a deep breath and focus on just one thing**.

This is useful for those moments that can be so **overwhelming** that it feels somewhat like an out-of-body experience – your consciousness disconnects from your senses, and it can often feel like you freeze, and time slows down as the situation washes over you.

In these moments, using this kind of grounding can help bring you back into the present – back into your body, so you can act and get things done.

Here you can think of some examples, such as:

- Feeling the weight of your equipment
- The texture of what you're holding
- The grip of your boots on the ground
- Or identifying one sound you can hear

ACTIVITY 5.1.3

In Step 1, what LB activation signs do you tend to notice in yourself that you can **use as signals** to use breathing?

....

....

....

....

....

....

....

....

....

....

Where can you, or have you used this technique?

....

....

....

....

....

....

....

....

....

....

ACTIVITY 5.1.4

What could be a grounding focus for you in the moment?

....

....

....

....

....

....

....

....

....

....

SCAN ME

Breathing in the **Driven Resilience App**

Scan the link to access the skill in the app (make sure you are **logged into the app first**).

app.hellodriven.com/activities/1235

NOTES

COMPOSURE

5.2

HIGH ADVERSITY REAPPRAISAL

5.2 HIGH ADVERSITY REAPPRAISAL

Learing Outcomes:

- Develop the ability to shift perspectives
- Learn how to change default emotional responses
- Provides 3 simple steps for using the technique

This is Useful For:

- Building motivation and drive when facing very difficult situations
- Reinterpret situations you faced in the past to be more constructive

We learned in the Thoughts & Behaviors skill about how your beliefs influence your emotions and behaviors. Now we can extend this further into exploring the more conscious approach you choose to interpret situations, since this determines how they will affect you.

In this skill, we'll talk about how you can **consciously shift perspective** on some of the challenges you might face in your work. This technique helps teach your brain to take a more constructive outlook on life and the situations you encounter.

5.2.1 Exploring Interpretations

Some common challenges might be:

- Stressed about **constant crises**
- Tired due to working **long hours** without much sleep
- Drained from **high workloads**
- Worn down from **little time to eat**, rest, or exercise
- Feeling lonely from **little time so socialize** and spend time with people

Of course, managing tough situations are your job. But just because it's your job doesn't mean it isn't going to affect you. These challenges are present for most in these lines of work, and it's crucial to be proactive rather than have them accumulate in your mind over time unmanaged.

Classes of Emotions

Experiences tend to have emotional reactions attached to them. Some might result in a very strong reaction to come up quickly when you read through different challenges.

Being able to **classify emotional responses** helps us better use these as data points so we can **decide what is best to do about them**.

As we saw before, we can map emotions across two scales:

- **Pleasure to displeasure** – Emotions to the right are generally preferable to the ones on the left. For example, people would rather feel joy than fear
- **Intensity** – This scale shows low energy emotions at the bottom (like boredom, calmness) up toward high energy emotions (rage, ecstasy)

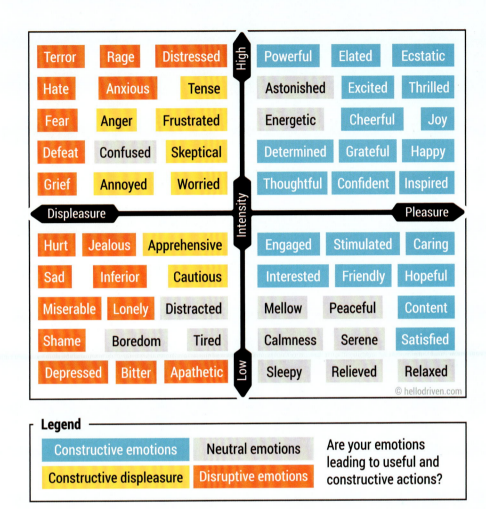

Terror	Rage	Distressed		Powerful	Elated	Ecstatic
Hate	Anxious	Tense		Astonished	Excited	Thrilled
Fear	Anger	Frustrated		Energetic	Cheerful	Joy
Defeat	Confused	Skeptical		Determined	Grateful	Happy
Grief	Annoyed	Worried		Thoughtful	Confident	Inspired

Displeasure — Intensity — **Pleasure**

Hurt	Jealous	Apprehensive		Engaged	Stimulated	Caring
Sad	Inferior	Cautious		Interested	Friendly	Hopeful
Miserable	Lonely	Distracted		Mellow	Peaceful	Content
Shame	Boredom	Tired		Calmness	Serene	Satisfied
Depressed	Bitter	Apathetic		Sleepy	Relieved	Relaxed

© hellodriven.com

Legend

- Constructive emotions
- Neutral emotions
- Constructive displeasure
- Disruptive emotions

Are your emotions leading to useful and constructive actions?

From there we can break them down into four broad classes of emotions:

- **Constructive emotions –** These are generally more pleasant emotions that are helpful and good for wellbeing
- **Neutral emotions –** These generally don't motivate specific behaviors as they lack clear direction within themselves
- **Disruptive emotions –** Generally unpleasant emotions that are not helpful for resilience or wellbeing because they reduce your ability to think clearly
- **Constructive displeasure emotions –** These are strong motivators, but need to be actively guided to be useful

By splitting them up this way, it helps us to classify and label the emotions we feel more accurately.

We can bring back to the emotion chart we used before, and now we can classify the emotions according to these four types.

- We see the **Constructive emotions** towards the Pleasure or Frontal Cortex side on the right. **Disruptive emotions** tend towards the Displeasure or Limbic side on the left
- **Neutral emotions** and **Constructive Displeasure** are generally around the middle.

As an example on the last one, **anger** can be useful, like getting angry at the dishes means you do them quickly to get it done. If you're in a **rage**, you might smash the dishes on the floor. One outcome here is much more constructive than the other.

Recalling what we learned in Reasoning in Optimizing Thoughts & Behaviors, the beliefs we have result in emotional reactions. Now you can start to see where those emotions end up on this chart and can have a big impact on how you feel and operate in your work and outside of it

ACTIVITY 5.2.1

Write down one challenge you are facing right now, and how do you feel about it?

....

....

....

....

....

....

....

....

....

....

....

....

SCAN ME

 # TECHNIQUE

Label Emotions

Need help naming a feeling? Scan the code below to use a step-by-step technique to label an emotion in the Driven Resilience App.

PS – make sure you are logged into your app to access this technique.

app.hellodriven.com/activities/150

5.2.2 Instinctive Reactions

Thinking back to the neuroscience part, the **limbic brain tends to try to protect you** through producing negative emotions like fear, anxiety, and sadness. This is a way to remind itself that it doesn't want to face those situations again. In other words, it's a technique the brain uses to try to **avoid situations**.

Instinctive responses come from facing some situation that then triggers beliefs. These beliefs determine your interpretation of a situation, which results in a mental response. For example:

1. You get pulled into another training session

2. You're already worn down from the last two days of training, triggering a belief that this is more training than what's needed

3. The result is you feel drained, and your attention drops during the training

Here you can see how the training session was interpreted into something negative, and a feeling of defeat followed that impacted performance.

PEOPLE WITH A NEGATIVE INTERPRETATION BIAS ARE **SIX TIMES MORE LIKELY** TO SHOW SYMPTOMS OF DEPRESSION.

Changing Interpretations

When it is your job to deal with difficult situations, you need to train your brain to keep your performance sustainable. This training to **change instinctive reactions into positive (helpful) responses** takes practice. It's natural for us to have certain tendencies in how we interpret events that are in themselves not necessarily positive or negative. Tendencies can lean towards negative interpretations, neutral, and positive. For example:

- **Generally negative interpretations –** You receive a message and immediately think *"Ugh, what is this now"*
- **Generally neutral interpretations –** You receive a message and read without any positive or negative expectations
- **Generally positive interpretations –** You receive a message and immediately think *"Ah a message, let's go!"*

Interpretation bias

Why is this bias important? Research found that people in high adversity occupations with a negative interpretation bias are six times more likely to show symptoms of depression[5].

Therefore, being able to shift your interpretation of situations can be a powerful skill that is protective of your mental strength over time.

Thinking back to the three types of challenges, consider how this skill could help with these:

- **Operational challenges** are relatively easier to interpret as important and worthwhile, since this is generally why do this job in the first place
- **Organizational challenges** can be harder – like being able to see paperwork as important, same with working shifts, and so on. This is where we need to apply deliberate effort to manage our interpretation of these things, but also being realistic in case there's a change we also need to push for in the environment itself
- **Relational challenges** can take more effort to manage our interpretation

So, how do you shift interpretation?

5   B. Kleim, H.A. Thörn, U. Ehlert, "Positive interpretation bias predicts well-being in medical interns" Front Psychol, 2014.

NOTES

1. Reinterpret the situation into **something positive**

2. Shift your emotional responses to be **more constructive**

3. Give yourself **evidence to believe it** – make it real

5.2.3 Reinterpreting Situations

The technique we'll be looking at is called **Reappraisal** and there are three key steps:

1. Reinterpret the situation into **something positive** like a challenge or opportunity

2. Reappraise your emotional response to be **more constructive**

3. Give yourself **evidence to believe it**

Following each step reinforces a new way of thinking and trains your brain. Doing so reduces impulsive brain activation while increasing prefrontal cortex activation, meaning your problem-solving skills improve and you can focus better on the task. Therefore, this not only builds mental strength, but it also **improves your effectiveness on the job**.

NOTES

....

....

....

....

....

....

....

....

....

....

To be clear, problems don't solve themselves just by thinking more positively. The goal of this technique is to put you in a more constructive mindset so that you become more effective at solving problems and taking productive action.

Let's explore each step in more detail.

1. Reinterpret the Situation

The key concept here is to re-think every problem, issue, or crisis and turn it into a challenge or opportunity. A 'challenge' is a test of your abilities. Succeeding or overcoming a challenge is exciting and builds confidence. That's why challenges are more positive than an issue.

The type of language you use in your own mind affects your motivation and emotional responses.

The thing about this technique is that it is useful in just about any difficult situation.

Here are some examples:

- Disagreement with your partner? Great opportunity to understand each other better
- Stuck in traffic? Great chance to listen to some music
- Car broke down? Great time to learn more about the mechanics of a car
- Can't get a dinner reservation? Great chance to think of more creative things to do
- Getting called into another crisis after not sleeping for two days? Great chance to see how far your body can go, and be proud when you're done (as well as learn when to say No)
- Made a big mistake at work? Great chance to reflect on what went wrong, learn, and improve
- Lost a friend in the line of duty, or to suicide? This is a reminder to look after yourself, proactively support others, and remember the good times you had with your friend

It can take some creative thinking. Not just that, **it can require courage and humility** to reinterpret some situations.

That's not to say some situations won't still be extremely painful. Though through changing your thinking you can turn those emotions into something more constructive.

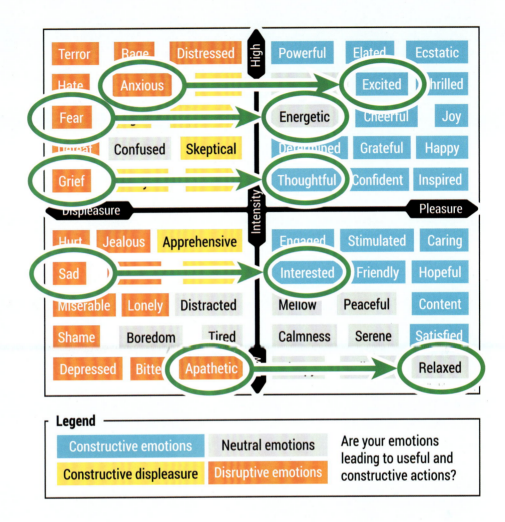

Legend

Constructive emotions	Neutral emotions	
Constructive displeasure	Disruptive emotions	

Are your emotions leading to useful and constructive actions?

2. Reappraising Emotional Responses

The second step is to determine your emotional reaction to an event and shift it to a more constructive emotion.

This means figuring out what emotion you're feeling in the first place. You can use the chart from before to help with this step.

Expanding on the four types of emotions we explored before, here are ideas to reappraise them:

- **Constructive emotions –** These are generally the ones we like to have and involve more prefrontal cortex activation, meaning they tend to motivate useful action that leads to us doing things that improve our situation and the world around us

- **Neutral emotions –** These in themselves don't necessarily mean anything, and can easily be reappraised (e.g. Astonished to Thrilled, Confused to Determined, Distracted to Content, Boredom to Satisfied)

- **Constructive displeasure –** Use the energy from these emotions to shift towards something useful (e.g. Anger to Energetic, Anxious to Excited, Worried to Thoughtful, Skeptical to Determined)

- **Disruptive displeasure –** These tend to work against us and mainly activate the limbic brain. These are important to shift towards being more constructive (e.g. Sad to Hopeful, Grief to Thoughtful, Defeat to Determined)

Using the emotion chart makes it easy to identify what you're feeling. Simply look at the chart, figure out which quadrant you are in, then look through the emotions to see which one feels right. Over time you won't need the chart anymore.

Once you've identified how you feel about a situation, next is to reappraise the emotion to something constructive. Here's the trick – **reappraise the emotion on the same intensity level.**

This part is important, since shifting to an emotion of a similar level of intensity feels authentic, because the physical sensations are very similar. For example, Anxious and Excited have similar sensations, while Anxious and Sleepy are two very different energy levels.

Reviewing the scenarios from before:

- Disagreement with your partner? Shift from **Anger to Determined** to get through this together
- Stuck in traffic? Shift from **Frustration to Gratitude** for the chance to listen to music
- Car broke down? Shift from feeling **Defeated to feeling Confident** in your ability to manage the problem
- Can't get a dinner reservation? Shift from feeling **Miserable towards feeling Interested** to find something different
- Getting called into another crisis after not sleeping for two days? Shift from **Annoyance to Determination** to get through the work
- Made a big mistake at work? Shift from **Shame to Hopeful** about being able to learn and improve your skills
- Lost a friend in the line of duty, or to suicide? Over time turn that extreme **Grief and Sadness into awareness and Gratitude.** Feeling grateful that you knew your friend, for the times you had, and gratitude for the life you and the people around you still have

Now that we've reappraised the situations and emotional responses, there's one step left.

NOTES

....
....
....
....
....
....
....
....
....
....
....
....
....
....
....

3. Give Yourself Evidence

Here it's important to come up with a reason for why the situation is truly an opportunity that you feel good about. The more convincing the reason, the more this technique will come together and lift your motivation and effectiveness.

One of the classic examples here was from research done on this technique. Researchers told two groups of people that they each had to do a public presentation on a topic[6].

People are naturally nervous about public speaking, however:

- For the **first group** the researchers just told them that this will be an important presentation and their performance will be graded
- For the **second group** the researcher told them to do the reappraisal technique – thinking about what a great opportunity this is to practice speaking, meeting people interested in the topic, what great experience it will be, and so on

The outcome was that the second group of speakers **enjoyed** the event a lot more. Not only that, but audience members also gave the second group **higher performance scores** than the first. This showed that not only does reappraisal help you enjoy a challenge, but also improves actual effectiveness, because reappraisal provides more blood flow to the prefrontal cortex, which helps you take control and perform at your best.

The key though is to give reasons for why it's a good opportunity or challenge. Having solid answers for this 'why' question helps to silence doubts later on. That's when you truly shift your mindset and perform at your best.

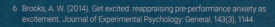

6 Brooks, A. W. (2014). Get excited: reappraising pre-performance anxiety as excitement. Journal of Experimental Psychology: General, 143(3), 1144.

A few interesting notes from this research:

- Shifting feeling anxious to excited **resulted in better performance than trying to 'calm down'** (since there's too much energy to feel calm). We often try to tell people who are stressed to just calm down, though it seems doing this doesn't work as well

- Most people do not think about shifting to excitement, and try to calm down instead, even though **calming down is not an effective strategy** when dealing with high energy negative emotions

This is why shifting horizontally across the mood chart works better – the authenticity of the emotion is maintained, and the evidence you provide to yourself about the new emotion backs up the feeling.

Ongoing practice of reappraisal can fundamentally change your life. **When you can find a positive aspect to every single thing that happens, then you gain a sense of excitement about the world that no one can take away from you.**

SCAN ME

TECHNIQUE

Reappraisal

Scan the code below to use a step-by-step reappraisal technique in the Driven Resilience App.

PS – make sure you are logged into your app to access this technique.

app.hellodriven.com/activities/152

ACTIVITY 5.2.2

Scenario – you get a message on your phone. Before looking at it, what is your first thought?

....

....

....

....

....

....

....

....

....

....

Explore what you wrote – is your first thought mostly positive, neutral, or negative?

....

....

....

....

....

....

....

....

....

ACTIVITY 5.2.3

Practice Reappraisal.

1. Reinterpret the situation into **something positive**

2. Shift your emotional responses to be **more constructive**

3. Give yourself **evidence to believe it** – make it real

Terror	Rage	Distressed	Powerful	Elated	Ecstatic
Hate	Anxious	Tense	Astonished	Excited	Thrilled
Fear	Anger	Frustrated	Energetic	Cheerful	Joy
Defeat	Confused	Skeptical	Determined	Grateful	Happy
Grief	Annoyed	Worried	Thoughtful	Confident	Inspired

High / **Intensity** / **Low**

Displeasure — **Pleasure**

Hurt	Jealous	Apprehensive	Engaged	Stimulated	Caring
Sad	Inferior	Cautious	Interested	Friendly	Hopeful
Miserable	Lonely	Distracted	Mellow	Peaceful	Content
Shame	Boredom	Tired	Calmness	Serene	Satisfied
Depressed	Bitter	Apathetic	Sleepy	Relieved	Relaxed

© hellodriven.com

Legend

- Constructive emotions
- Neutral emotions
- Constructive displeasure
- Disruptive emotions

Are your emotions leading to useful and constructive actions?

Take the challenge you wrote down in Activity 5.1. Do **Step 1.** What is a more positive or constructive way to think about the situation?

....
....
....
....
....
....
....

Next, do **Step 2.** What is the current emotion you are feeling about it? Which constructive emotion can you shift towards that is on a similar level of intensity?

....
....
....
....
....
....
....
....
....

Finally **Step 3.** What evidence can you give yourself to back up the reappraised situation and emotion?

....
....
....
....
....
....
....
....
....

High Adversity Reappraisal in the **Driven Resilience App**

Scan the link to access the skill in the app (make sure you are **logged into the app** first).

app.hellodriven.com/activities/1236

TENACITY

PR6 RESILIENCE DOMAIN

6.1

MENTAL LOAD MANAGEMENT

6.1 MENTAL LOAD MANAGEMENT

The work you do puts unique pressures on your mental wellbeing. This section explores four specific types of challenges you might face from a mental perspective, focusing on recognizing the signs and **building proactive resilience to each of these**.

This is where we focus on a strength-based approach, where ideally you aim to:

- Maintain a **high level of engagement** and enjoyment of what you do
- **Enjoy your role as a carer**, or someone who helps others
- Develop **resilience to vicarious stresses** you might face
- And develop **resilience towards otherwise traumatic experiences**

With each we'll take time to understand what it is, look at signs & symptoms, and strategies for preventative and reactive action.

These are important skills, not just in terms of looking after yourself, but also for looking after those that you work with. Try to look at the content from this perspective so that you build up your knowledge, similar to the Resilience First Aid program.

6.1.1 Maintaining Engagement

Let's explore what high engagement looks like and compare it to its opposite form, which is called burnout.

When you are highly engaged with your work, then work doesn't feel like work. Signs of **high engagement** include:

- You are **interested** in what you do, finding it easy to focus and get things done
- You are *keen* to take on new tasks and challenges
- You feel **dedicated** and enthusiastic about your work
- You feel **involved** and enjoy working with those around you
- You feel **productive** and that you are making an important contribution
- You feel **proud** and have a sense of accomplishment about the work you do

This is a great place to be in – a spot that's genuinely enjoyable and fulfilling. These aspects of engagement contrast with what we looked at before about **Job Satisfaction** where it's more about the environment itself, such as leadership, management support, opportunities for growth, etc. Those are more external factors about your work, where engagement is more about factors internal to yourself.

Burnout

The opposite of engagement is burnout where you might see physical, emotional, and behavioral symptoms:

Physical symptoms

- Feeling exhausted and tired most of the time
- Headaches and frequently becoming ill
- Trouble sleeping
- Changes in eating habits

Emotional symptoms

- Feeling cynical about the work and the future
- Self-doubt and feeling like a failure
- Feeling alone and detached
- Lacking motivation

Behavioral symptoms

- Procrastinating and being slow to respond
- Increased use of escapism (apps, tv shows that take your mind off things, etc)
- Frustration at others and more negativity in communication
- Avoiding responsibilities and tasks
- Withdrawing from interaction with people
- Using food, alcohol, caffeine, or other substances to cope

Engagement vs Burnout

There is a **continuum between Engagement and Burnout**.

On the positive end, you really enjoy your work, it energizes you and you are keen to do more. On the other end, you might feel exhausted and cynical. Or, as is usually the case, you might be in the middle range.

With burnout, prevention is best, so it's worth exploring risk factors. Once you understand these more, then we can explore strategies you can use to move back into a feeling of engagement.

ACTIVITY 6.1.1

Risk factors of burnout

What puts us at risk of burning out in the first place? Let's take a look – tick off the ones you notice in yourself.

Personal Factors

Certain personalities are more likely to burn out than others. For example:

☐ **Perfectionists** are more likely to burn out due to extreme high standards they put on themselves

☐ **People pleasers** who try to be everything for everyone are at higher risk as there are always more people that need something

☐ **High achievers** are more at risk due to not taking enough time to look after themselves and refuel along the way

☐ **Value conflict** is another of factor. For example, someone who becomes a veterinarian because they love animals might get disillusioned when it turns out their job is mostly about putting down animals, going against values of helping and caring

☐ **Caring for others**, especially if constant, takes a toll

Organizational Stress

Various pressures from your organization can add to burnout, including:

☐ Constant **work overload**

☐ **Unreasonable deadlines** and time pressure

☐ **Not having enough control** over your work, or lack of clarity in your role

☐ **Unfair treatment**

☐ **Lack of communication**

☐ **Lack of rewards** and recognition

☐ **Extremes of work**, where it may either be too monotonous or too chaotic

These can wear down your personal resources over time, gradually adding up to a feeling of overload and burnout.

Being Deeply Invested

☐ The original researchers looking into burnout heard people say how they used to be "on fire" meaning they were keen, had lots of energy, and they really cared about what they do and who they help. Eventually they felt like that fire burned out, like there was no more fuel left and they were left exhausted. That's where the concept of 'burnout' came from.

Here the key point is that the burned-out workers used to **really care about their work**. In a way, they would not have burned out if they were never really invested. However, not caring brings other problems.

The point then is that the fire in yourself is something to sustain. Now and then you need to add more fuel back into the tank to keep the fire going.

YOU CAN'T KEEP RACING IF YOU NEVER REFUEL.

This is where a simple way to think of it is in terms of maintaining and **refueling yourself**. Just like any high-performance sports car or athlete, you can't keep racing if you never refuel.

To maintain your own high performance, you need to look after yourself. While some levels of stress are useful, it's important to recognize when it becomes too much.

A high level of engagement is where we'd like to be, though sometimes factors lead us to where we experience burnout. Burnout is very common in high adversity roles, because:

▲ Many in these occupations **identify very strongly** with their role

▲ Workdays tend to be **chaotic and unpredictable**

▲ Workloads tend to be high with **long shifts and work hours**

▲ **High expectations** placed on themselves and a tendency to internalize failures

Burnout generally starts with being under **constant high stress**, though burnout is quite different from stress itself. Let's set these two apart.

Stress & Burnout

Stress is generally a result of there being too much pressure, too many things to do, too many deadlines, too many expectations. This can result in physical damage to your health if it goes on too long.

Burnout is more about there being not enough. You don't have energy, don't have the drive to start things, you feel drained and hopeless.

With stress, it feels like if you can just get things done, then things will be better. With burnout, it's hard to even care anymore.

The diagram shows a comparison of the differences between stress and burnout.

This is also where stress is often easier to notice than burnout, which is where self-assessments are useful, as well as keeping an eye out for your team members.

SCAN ME

QUICK TEST

Engagement

Scan the code below to complete a short assessment to measure your current levels of engagement at work.

You can do this assessment again later to see how your skill changes over time.

PS – make sure you are logged into your app to access this assessment.

app.hellodriven.com/activities/852

STRESS

- ABOUT 'TOO MUCH' -
- HIGH EFFORT -
- OVERREACTIVE EMOTIONS -
- HYPERACTIVITY -
- PHYSICAL DAMAGE -
- RISK OF ANXIETY -

BURNOUT

- ABOUT 'TOO LITTLE'
- LOW EFFORT
- BLUNTED EMOTIONS
- HOPELESSNESS
- EMOTIONAL DAMAGE
- RISK OF DEPRESSION

ACTIVITY 6.1.2

Take notes on strategies you are using or can use.

Strategies to Maintain High Engagement

In many ways, you are like a high-performance race car. As you race, you need to stop now and then to refuel and do maintenance. Without this, you can't keep racing.

This is basically what it means to be able to avoid burnout and maintain high engagement where you enjoy your work and can sustain high performance.

Keep Perspective About Work

The way you think about your work is important.

☐ **Take pressure off yourself –** If you're a high achiever or have perfectionist tendencies, allow yourself to make mistakes without beating yourself up. Focus on learning without judging yourself

☐ **Change how you look at problems –** In the Reappraisal technique we talk about how to reframe the challenges you face. Keep practicing this technique to embed a healthy mindset

☐ **Remember the good stuff –** Your job is one where you likely place heavy focus on things that went wrong. The Three Good Things technique is a useful one to train your brain to also remember things that went well, helping you notice the things that make it worth it

☐ **Don't sacrifice everything –** When you really care about your work, it's easy to sacrifice everything you can for it. But if you sacrifice too much, there might not be anything left to give

Keep in mind that work is one part of life. It's not everything. Even if what you do is really important, you need to look after yourself first so you can do your work well.

☐ **Have a Resilient Vision**

If you identify strongly with your work, take care that your job isn't your ultimate goal. For example, if your purpose is to "Be a firefighter" then you put yourself at risk, because if something happens that means you can't do that job anymore, then you have a loss of identity.

This also means that if something threatens that purpose, you'll be extremely stressed by it.

Instead, a resilient vision (or purpose) is something at a higher level that is more general. For example, your resilient vision might be "To help people" and your work as a firefighter is only how you currently achieve that vision.

The difference here is that if something happens and you can't work as a firefighter anymore, you can still help people in other ways. Maybe you can train other

Manage Organizational Stress

A big factor that influences burnout is organizational stress. These are often things outside your direct control, though how you respond to it is under your control:

☐ **Manage up –** Your managers and supervisors are there to help you do your job well. If something isn't working for you, tell them about it and come up with a solution that they can easily approve

☐ **Lead the leaders –** If you are not happy with leadership, practice your diplomacy skills by letting leaders know what you are hoping to see from them (again, be diplomatic about this)

☐ **Don't overload yourself –** Only take on extra work if you truly have capacity. If not, build confidence to say no

☐ **Get ahead of change –** There's always change in staff and structures. Get ahead of it by instigating change through identifying new roles you want and pushing for it

☐ **Create your own development opportunities –** Rather than wait for management to give you a change for development, find things you want to learn and make a case for why they should support you to get trained

If it's too broken, move on – Sometimes you may come across toxic environments. If it's something you simply can't work with, move on

It's not all up to you, though often you have more control than you may initially realize. Part of the challenge here is to understand the intricacies of the workplace well enough so you can play a constructive role. Put yourself first so you can do your work well.

Connect With People

One of the most important parts is to stay connected with people!

☐ **Make friends** at work and maintain them through purposeful contact

☐ Have fun with your work teams and **use humor** in different ways to lighten the work

☐ Invest in friendships and relationships **outside work** where you can

☐ **Talk about what's causing stress** at work and what's been happening lately

☐ Also **talk about things not work-related** so you can take a mental break

☐ **Limit contact with negative** people who bring you down or drain your energy

Keeping these relationships going will help you enjoy work more overall and increase your resilience to the stresses you might face.

Manage Your Health

Being able to maintain your discipline with health is a good way to keep your mind in top shape as well.

☐ **Exercise regularly –** Four proper workout sessions a week is great

☐ **Eat healthy foods –** Avoid sugary treats, fast food and processed foods

☐ **Avoid using alcohol, caffeine or substances to cope –** Rather try to get good rest and keep things natural where possible

☐ **Maintain good sleep –** As best you can, get good sleep. If you do shift work & long hours, use the strategies in the Work Hours tutorials.

Often if you struggle with these, it's a sign of burnout starting to happen.

Which strategies can you implement?

◢...
◢...
◢...
◢...
◢...
◢...
◢...
◢...
◢...
◢...
◢...
◢...
◢...
◢...
◢...
◢...
◢...
◢...
◢...
◢...

QUICK TEST

Carer Satisfaction

Scan the code below to complete a short assessment to explore your current satisfaction levels with providing care and supporting others.

You can do this assessment again later to see how your skill changes over time. PS – make sure you are logged into your app to access this assessment.

app.hellodriven.com/activities/873

NOTES

....
....
....
....
....
....
....
....
....
....
....
....
....

6.1.2 Carer Satisfaction

The concept of **carer satisfaction** is about how fulfilling you find your role as a carer (someone who cares for or supports others, which can be at work or at home). Usually this is one of the most meaningful aspects of the job, though caring can come at a cost.

Continuing with the theme of mental load, this **cost of caring** needs to be managed well to be able to maintain the satisfaction you get from caring for people.

Being able to find a path towards a higher level of satisfaction with caring can be helpful if you plan to have a long career in your field. Otherwise, if you are experiencing a downwards trend here and having a harder time empathizing with people, then you might be heading towards **compassion fatigue**. This is important to recognize so that you can work on ways to reverse this trend.

High Carer Satisfaction

Compassion fatigue is essentially the opposite of carer satisfaction. Let's see what a high level of carer satisfaction looks like:

- You have a lot of **empathy and compassion** for people – the desire to help and ease their pain
- You **don't mind the procedures**, paperwork and protocols involved with caring or helping – you see their value
- You enjoy **seeing and interacting** with the people you help
- You **look forward** to seeing the people you help again
- You feel that you have an **abundance to give**, a desire to help

Usually this is what you experience early in your career, as this is exactly why most people go into work as carers. Over time, however, this can change.

Compassion Fatigue

Caring for others constantly comes at a cost. As before, if you don't stop and refuel now and then, this cost can eventually erode your ability to have empathy for people.

In this sense, compassion fatigue is essentially about losing your ability to care for and have compassion towards people. Let's look at some signs and symptoms. As we go through here, you may notice quite a bit of overlap with burnout, which is because these two often appear together.

Physical

▲ Difficulty sleeping, reduced sleep quality

▲ Physical exhaustion

▲ Feeling tense or easily agitated (higher limbic brain activation)

▲ Frequent headaches

Emotional

▲ Finding it hard to care about the pain someone else is feeling, sometimes being insensitive (thinking to yourself "Why are you complaining, I've heard much worse")

▲ Feeling overwhelmed or hypersensitive about suffering of others

▲ Hearing about the suffering of others make you feel hopeless or helpless

▲ Feeling detached from your surroundings

▲ Feeling numb, drained, or exhausted

▲ Feeling resentment towards the people you are helping, and feeling guilty about that since you're supposed to care about them

Behavioral

▲ Using food, alcohol, caffeine, or other substances to cope

▲ Lack of self-care and personal hygiene

▲ Getting complaints about your work or attitude

▲ Lower productivity or efficacy at work

▲ Withdrawing from people around you

Here burnout is mainly about exhaustion, compassion fatigue is more specifically about having **no resources left to be able to empathize and be compassionate towards people**.

The challenge is to maintain a sense of satisfaction with your role over time. Often people start out enthusiastic, only to become cold and jaded over time.

This can be difficult to deal with, as the very reason for why you started in this line of work is being eroded away.

When it comes to others you work with, you might notice these symptoms, especially behavioral ones. You might also hear them start to complain a lot more about their work and the people they help.

CARER SATISFACTION

VS

COMPASSION FATIGUE

ACTIVITY 6.1.3

Identify and tick off the risk that might apply to yourself.

Compassion Fatigue Risk Factors

Let's take a closer look now at what increases the risk of compassion fatigue developing.

☐ **Working mainly with extreme trauma** including physical and mental trauma patients. Beyond responders and healthcare workers, this also includes lawyers, investigators, counsellors, etc that review material like this

☐ **Strict procedural aspects** such as working with patients where you need to stay in uncomfortable personal protective equipment for long periods, or other rigid procedures enforced within the organization

☐ **Working with people with little or no hope** such as palliative (end of life) care or oncology where effort sometimes feel hopeless, including caring for elderly and family members

☐ **Jobs where injuries seem unnecessary** such as a paramedic working night shifts where most calls are alcohol-related, police working a 'bad' neighbourhood, or a nurse getting frustrated at cardiac disease patients unwilling to make lifestyle changes

☐ **Interacting with many** people increases risk as the large number of cases start to blend together. This includes working in a busy hospital, or military medics working in highly active areas with large numbers of casualties

☐ **Not having enough support** also contributes, placing additional pressure on you to get things done without others to take over some tasks along the way. Could also mean not having the equipment or tools to do your work

☐ **Unrelenting workloads** where there is never enough time to do all the work required and patients or cases keep coming in. This could be extremely demanding jobs where there are constant issues and crises coming up

☐ **No time for rest** such as when you are working a full-time job then also caring for a high-needs person at home that leaves you with no time for yourself or to even get proper sleep. Also applies to having newborns requiring constant attention through the night

Compassion fatigue in many ways is a defense mechanism of the brain to try and protect yourself from the constant experience of dealing with trauma.

Experiencing compassion fatigue is not a personal failure or a character flaw, but rather something that naturally happens. Even preventative care doesn't necessarily protect completely. Being aware of these risk factors and monitoring yourself over time is helpful to maintain a level of carer satisfaction.

NOTES

ACTIVITY 6.1.4

Compassion Fatigue Strategies

Take notes on what strategies you can use.

☐ Care For Yourself First

The most important step is a change in mindset about caring in general. Many people who get into roles where they help others are also the type of people that would gladly sacrifice everything to help someone else. From giving all their time through to taking a bullet for someone.

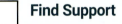

CARE **FIRST FOR YOURSELF** BEFORE CARING FOR OTHERS.

However, when it comes to being able to do this type of work sustainably, then you need to shift towards this mindset:

Also known as **the airplane principle** where you put your own oxygen mask on first before helping others. After all, you're no help if you are passed out on the floor while the plane is in trouble.

It might seem simple, but it can be difficult to switch to this mindset because:

- ◢ For many carers and helpers, helping is such a **deep part of their personality** that they easily switch back to old habits of giving too much as soon as they feel they are needed
- ◢ It **can feel selfish** to care for yourself when others are in need

However, it's not selfish to care for yourself. It's necessary. You can think of it from the perspective that even more people will suffer if you burn out and can't help them anymore.

It's better for the world overall if you spend a bit more time caring for yourself first so that you have more energy to care for others in a sustainable way.

Be realistic about your capabilities – you can't help everyone. You can't stop everyone's suffering, and if this is what you aim for you are setting yourself up for disappointment and a sense of failure. You do make a difference, but it's important to do it in a way that doesn't drain you over time. Finding this balance takes time and practice.

☐ Find Support

Don't suffer alone. Reach out to the support provided by your organization. Talk to a professional, contact helplines, talk to co-workers, any way you can start talking can help.

☐ Take a Holiday

Often people avoid holidays because they can't afford not getting paid for a few weeks, or feel they are too needed at work – but remember that burnout is serious and can have a major impact on being able to do your work at all. Make saving for and enjoying a few weeks off a priority so you can start to replenish yourself.

☐ Change Your Work

Talk to your manager, supervisor, or support personnel to see if there's something else you can do instead of what you currently do. A change like this might be the best to reinvigorate yourself.

Just as all of this applies to you, it also applies to your team and everyone around you. Use this knowledge not only to help look after yourself, but also to spot symptoms of burnout in others and support them back towards high engagement.

ACTIVITY 6.1.4 *cont.*

Keep an eye out, not just for yourself, but also those you work with.

....
....
....
....
....
....
....
....
....
....
....
....
....
....
....
....
....
....
....

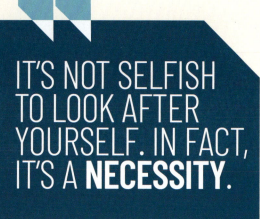

IT'S NOT SELFISH TO LOOK AFTER YOURSELF. IN FACT, IT'S A **NECESSITY**.

ACTIVITY 6.1.5

What's your experience with compassion fatigue? How do you maintain your enjoyment in helping?

....
....
....
....
....
....
....
....
....
....
....
....
....
....
....
....

6.1.3 Vicarious Resilience

Vicarious trauma was originally noticed in counsellors that work with trauma patients, where the repeated exposure to these stories and experiences of trauma started to affect the counsellors themselves.

However, the effects that these exposures can have are not just limited to trauma counsellors, as many other professions deal with these exposures as well.

Examples include:

- **Crisis call operators** repeatedly talking to people who have experienced something traumatic
- **Police and investigators** managing and reviewing cases of horrific crimes
- **EMTs, nurses and doctors** dealing with patients involved in abuse, intentional harm, or extreme injuries
- **Military personnel** hearing horror stories from other soldiers
- **Firefighters** reviewing terrible cases and hearing stories from others
- **Parents or partners** hearing about a traumatic experience of someone close to them

The list goes on. Professions that deal with this aspect of reality need to be able to contend with the effects of this type of secondary exposure, which is where vicarious resilience comes in.

High Vicarious Resilience

When you have a high level of resilience to vicarious exposure:

- You can keep repeated exposures to the traumatic experiences of others in **perspective** and you don't let it affect how you view the world
- You **don't notice any negative changes** in your habits, routines, or sleeping patterns due to your work
- You get a **sense of satisfaction** from the people you work with and feel hopeful for the future
- You stay active with **friendships and social connections** both inside and outside of work
- You can clearly **separate work from personal life** and are able to be calm and happy outside of work

To help understand this resilience more, it's useful to explore the effects and risk factors of vicarious trauma.

SCAN ME

QUICK TEST

Vicarious Exposure

Scan the code below to complete a short assessment to explore your current exposure to vicarious trauma.

You can do this assessment again later to see how your skill changes over time. PS – make sure you are logged into your app to access this assessment.

app.hellodriven.com/activities/1227

Effects of Vicarious Trauma

The effects of vicarious trauma are similar to experiencing direct trauma, except that the source is through an empathetic connection with someone else.

Perception changes

A key aspect of vicarious trauma is that it changes your perception and perspective of life and other people. Particularly, aspects **like trust, safety, esteem, intimacy, and control are negatively affected**.

ACTIVITY 6.1.6

Have you noticed your opinions of the world change in this way?

....

....

....

....

....

....

....

....

....

....

....

....

....

....

....

....

EXAMPLE

Shifting Frame of Reference

After hearing about traumatic experiences, you might become more wary of other people, seeing them as dangerous or becoming suspicious of them

Previously you might have been fine to chat to a stranger but suddenly you find yourself scared about what kind of person they might be, and you instead avoid talking to people

You start to avoid situations you used to enjoy because now you see danger everywhere, like going to a bar with a few friends because you heard of something terrible that happened to someone you work with

You find yourself losing faith in humanity after hearing about too many terrible things people do to each other

This kind of traumatic injury to your beliefs about the world is challenging to deal with, since it can feel like you now see the truth about how bad the world really is. Like your eyes have been opened and you now have a more 'realistic' view of life and the dangers of people and before you were naïve.

The problem here is that **thought distortions like overgeneralization and catastrophic thinking** have crept in, distorting your view of the world.

When your job constantly exposes you to the worst of life, that can become your frame of reference – you subconsciously assume that what you deal with is everywhere, when in reality that's only one small part of life and overall things are actually pretty good.

LIFE

GOOD STUFF

HARD STUFF

YOUR JOB

While this image might be a simplification, it can help to keep in mind there's still much about life that's outside of the work. Taking time to appreciate that and keep it separate from your work helps to maintain perspective.

To some degree it's ok for there to have been some change in your view about the world. Though it's when the degree of change is large, and you lose hope for the world and start withdrawing from it that it becomes a view to challenge.

Other Effects of Vicarious Trauma

Like burnout and compassion fatigue, the effects of experiencing this also cross emotional, behavioral, physical, and mental factors.

NOTES

....
....
....
....
....
....
....
....
....
....
....
....
....
....
....
....
....
....

Emotional

- Sadness, depression, anxiety
- Feelings of guilt, shame
- Easily frustrated
- Self-destructive thoughts
- Fluctuations in mood
- Changes in sense of humor

Behavioral

- Alcohol, caffeine, substances, eating
- Not exercising
- Avoiding people & activities you used to enjoy
- Risky behaviors – driving fast, take up gambling

Physical

- Struggling with sleep
- Frequent digestive issues
- Rashes, headaches
- Frequent illnesses, taking time off work
- Nervous energy
- Easily startled by noises

Mental

- Becoming negative, cynical, hopeless
- Losing sense of purpose
- Feeling disconnected
- Avoiding memories
- Having nightmares, flashbacks

ACTIVITY 6.1.7

Risk Factors for Vicarious Trauma

The higher your risk, the more vigilant it helps to be with maintaining vicarious resilience. But these risks are not just up to you - your organization also plays a part in supporting your resilience.

Type of Exposure

Given the nature of vicarious trauma, it shouldn't be a surprise that the type of trauma you deal with has different effects. For example:

- ☐ Working mainly with cases that involve **children** being harmed has a strong effect, given natural tendencies to feel protective towards children
- ☐ Working with people that have little or **no hope** for recovery, like terminal diseases, palliative care, etc
- ☐ Working with **severe mental illness** where the behavior of people can be disturbing, and suicide is common
- ☐ Working with **animals** where you witness the effects of abuse
- ☐ Being in an environment where you frequently hear about **terrifying situations** and actions, such as sexual assault investigations, intentional harm, etc that shake your faith in humanity
- ☐ Situations where actions are **heavily against your sense of right and wrong** such as 'fog of war' incidents in the military

In essence, the worse the exposure, and the more frequent the exposure, the higher the risk of vicarious trauma.

Organizational factors

The actual exposure to trauma is one factor. Another factor is one we talk about in the Connecting Purpose skill, which is about organizational factors. This includes:

- ☐ **Workload –** The risk of vicarious trauma increases with higher workload, especially if the exposure to traumatic experiences is increased. Further, if you tend to work long hours to the extent where work is your life, then it can make it more difficult to separate work from personal life and the experiences of those you work with become your main frame of reference
- ☐ **Wearing many hats –** If you have many different responsibilities including some where you must deal with other people and the issues they have, then that can further increase risk
- ☐ **Lack of support –** If you are mainly expected to deal with things by yourself and there aren't people around to help you with these kinds of challenges, then it's more likely to feel overwhelmed and hopeless about the stories you hear and people you work with
- ☐ **Negative environment –** If you have a negative view of leadership, bad experiences with management, conflict with co-workers, little recognition, etc, then it tends to wear down your ability to cope with these types of situations

This is where the structure of your organization plays a role in your ability to manage this type of stress. After all, **it's not just up to you** – it's also about your organization supporting you effectively.

....
....
....
....
....
....
....
....
....

ACTIVITY 6.1.8

Take notes on strategies you are using or can use.

Strategies to Build Vicarious Resilience

Ultimately, being conscious of this risk and taking active steps to build vicarious resilience is helpful in maintaining your ability to do your work in the long term. Here are some ideas. organization also plays a part in supporting your resilience.

Rebuild Perspective

A key factor about vicarious trauma is that it distorts your view of the world. Building and maintaining a healthy perspective is helpful. How does this work?

☐ **Challenge thought distortions –** In the Thoughts & Behaviors tutorial we talk about distortions and ways to challenge them. For example, assuming all people are dangerous might keep you safe, but it also means you miss out on many great relationships and situations because most people aren't dangerous

☐ **Use compartmenting strategies –** To help maintain a proper separation between the things you hear about at work and your private life, use the Compartmenting skill to keep perspective of your work as a small portion of life overall, and that there is much to be hopeful about

☐ **Recognize your challenges –** Sometimes people feel that they shouldn't be affected by their work since they haven't faced as much trauma as someone else. Though you are still human, and anyone that cares about people can be affected. Have empathy for yourself just as you do for others

Focus on Small Wins

☐ People who work with trauma patients often find that acknowledging small wins helps them maintain hope through difficult work.

This can be something tiny, like a suggestion you made to someone that they followed through on, or someone thanking you for something you helped them with.

The Three Good Things technique in this program specifically helps to build this habit. After all, the key is to actually note down these good things and small wins – this focus will help you find hope even in the toughest situations.

Structural Support

A highly supportive environment is a key ingredient to enhancing vicarious resilience. Again, here it's not just about you being able to deal with everything all by yourself. Your organization needs to support your resilience. This means:

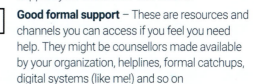

☐ **Good formal support –** These are resources and channels you can access if you feel you need help. They might be counsellors made available by your organization, helplines, formal catchups, digital systems (like me!) and so on

☐ **Good informal support –** These are your co-workers, peer support groups, and so on. Having work friends, you can talk to and share the harder parts of the job with is an important source of strength

☐ **Good supervision –** If you work with patients, having a supervisor you can turn to for tough cases can be very helpful. Especially when you feel they are affecting you more than usual

Of course, support being available doesn't really mean anything if you're not willing to use them. If you find it hard to personally recognize when you should be talking to someone, then doing the Vicarious Resilience Check now and then can help. Look for if your scores go down, or if you score at a moderate or low level.

....

....

....

....

....

Personal Strategies

Doing activities that help separate work from personal time are helpful to give you breathing room so you can recharge. These include:

☐ Leisure activities   ☐ Mindfulness

☐ Regular exercise   ☐ Social activities

☐ Healthy eating   ☐ Using humor

You might think doing all these is a lot, though being able to engage in them is a good indicator you have a higher level of vicarious resilience. If you stop engaging in these then that's a sign to reach out and chat to someone.

Situation Debriefs

☐ Another way to work through the impact of certain cases and incidents is to use debriefs. These can be fast, taking only a few minutes to focus on what happened, what worked and what can be improved. Or they could be longer sessions facilitated with groups of people to walk through an incident in more detail.

There are mixed views in terms of the usefulness of debriefs, though what is important is that debriefs take a constructive and safe approach that doesn't cause more harm than good.

When dealing with things you heard, cases you're working on, and so on, you might not have easy access to debriefs for all those times. An option there is to use the **Digital Situation Debrief** option available in the HART course in the **Driven Resilience App**.

This is available for you to work through any time by yourself to look at different aspects of a situation and help you process it mentally. With that option you can choose a short version, or a more detailed version. You can access it by scanning the code below:

(app.hellodriven.com/activities/845)

Identify three strategies you can invest in more to build vicarious resilience:

◢...
◢...
◢...
◢...
◢...
◢...
◢...
◢...
◢...
◢...
◢...
◢...
◢...
◢...
◢...
◢...
◢...
◢...
◢...
◢...
◢...
◢...
◢...

6.1.4   Trauma Resilience

Going beyond vicarious trauma, now we shift towards direct exposure to extreme events. In research, this is generally referred to as exposure to Potentially Traumatic Events (PTE's). That is to say, the events are extreme, and won't necessarily cause trauma, though the exposures have the potential to be experienced as traumatic.

While you need to manage the impact of extreme experiences yourself, it also helps to understand better the effect the situation might have on others you work with or support.

What is Trauma Resilience?

Trauma resilience means:

- **You Are Informed** – You know about trauma, its effects, what it might lead to, as well as ways to deal with its effects
- **You Are Prepared** – You do exercises that actively help build resilience and prepares your brain so that you can resist the negative effects of experiencing trauma
- **You Are Fast to Respond** – You can quickly recognize when you do show negative effects so that you can respond effectively and work through them – the ability to put your knowledge into action

There's no reliable way that you can totally avoid all the negative effects of experiencing extreme events. Through these steps, you can start to build your resilience specifically in relation to experiencing traumatic situations.

First, let's focus on becoming more informed.

Trauma in the Brain

Previously we talked about the limbic brain. Situations that heavily violate our sense of safety activate an **extreme reaction in the amygdala** which is the part in the limbic brain that constantly scans for danger. This could be due to a situation that threatens you or someone you care about. This reaction is stronger the less prepared the brain is for the event.

The amygdala activates the hippocampus which controls memory formation. The problem here is that the hippocampus is activated so strongly, that it **creates a traumatic memory** which is connected to all kinds of sights, sounds, smells, and thoughts experienced at that moment.

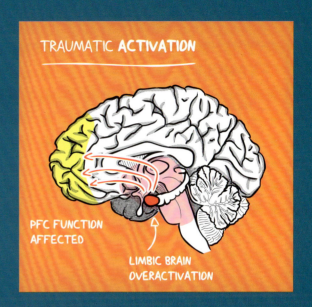

TRAUMATIC **ACTIVATION**

PFC FUNCTION AFFECTED

LIMBIC BRAIN OVERACTIVATION

The brain is trying to record as much detail about the situation as quickly as possible so that it can 'help' you avoid similar situations in the future.

Along with that, the **limbic brain quickly changes wiring to the prefrontal cortex** (PFC) which causes you to have less conscious control of when this traumatic memory activates again, to some extent the LB tries to automate your avoidance of a similar situation occurring.

In essence, during exposure to a traumatic event, the brain:

1. **Activates** the limbic brain very strongly
2. **Records** as much detail as possible
3. **Adapts** the brain to avoid similar situations in the future

While the brain might mean well, it doesn't do this very well in a modern world where situations are complex. Especially with reducing the functioning of the PFC, which means it becomes harder to think clearly when something activates that experience.

EXAMPLE

Sunset Experience

For example, let's say Sandy nearly died during a rock-climbing accident at sunset. In the future sunsets might activate severe fear. This might then cause her to avoid sunsets – staying inside with curtains closed so she wouldn't notice when the sun is setting.

Sunsets had nothing really to do with the event, though the brain took in everything related to the event and connected painful memories these different aspects in a somewhat misguided effort to avoid similar danger in the future.

Mental Trauma as Biological Injury

In many ways, trauma such as Post-traumatic Stress Injury (PTSI) is a biological injury. You can think of it like fracturing your forearm. If left to heal by itself, it might set incorrectly, causing ongoing pain and your hand might not work properly. **It needs to be treated** so it sets properly, and you can get full use back of your hand.

The bone isn't 'wrong' for having broken. It's just that the situation placed too much stress on it. **Just like a person isn't 'wrong' for getting PTSI.** The situation just overloaded the limbic brain, and now there is some wiring that needs to be treated.

You can strengthen a bone through regular exercise and practice to be stronger and be less likely to break. After a bone break, a properly treated bone heals back stronger than it was before. Again, it's very similar to the mind – **you can train your brain to resist trauma, and properly working through trauma can make you stronger than you were before.**

Besides, breaking a bone is often a sign that you are out there and living your life. Pretty much the only way to avoid breaks like that is to avoid life.

This is often a defense mechanism that appears after trauma – avoidance is one of the first psychological challenges to overcome to get back to living life.

NOTES

....
....
....
....
....
....
....
....
....
....
....
....
....
....

EXAMPLE

Tetris & Trauma

Flashbacks and intrusive memories are a difficult part of dealing with trauma. Though the way that the brain stores those powerful memories that produce flashbacks is a process that can be disrupted.

Researchers gave car crash survivors Tetris to play while they wait in the emergency room[7]. What they found was that those who played Tetris had a 62% lower chance of experiencing flashbacks.

Why? Tetris is a visually demanding game, and playing it shortly after a traumatic event distracts the brain, meaning the brain has less resources available to create highly powered memories that produce flashbacks.

It's fascinating that knowing more about the brain can help us uncover useful tricks like this.

7   Iyadurai, L., Blackwell, S. E., Meiser-Stedman, R., Watson, P. C., Bonsall, M. B., Geddes, J. R., ... & Holmes, E. A. (2018). Preventing intrusive memories after trauma via a brief intervention involving Tetris computer game play in the emergency department: a proof-of-concept randomized controlled trial. *Molecular psychiatry*, 23(3), 674-682.

Signs of Traumatic Injury

Most people have some kind of traumatic experience somewhere during their life. Usually we get through it ok, though sometimes the injury is of a scale that requires additional effort to work through.

Post-traumatic stress injury (PTSI) is when there is a specific set of signs and symptoms that are used to make a clinical diagnosis. The full criteria to diagnose PTSI is complex and requires a professional to conduct a full assessment and develop a diagnosis.

Something to keep in mind is that most people don't meet all the criteria of a diagnosis following traumatic exposure. Though, that doesn't mean they are unaffected.

Instead, someone might experience some symptoms which might still make life somewhat difficult. For example, after Sandy's rock-climbing incident, she might avoid hanging out with her climbing friends, since being around them reminds her of the event. Over time her circle of friends might shrink and feel more and more lonely and isolated. This means there's still something for her to work on to not let the event hold her back.

On the other hand, exposure to trauma doesn't necessarily mean you'll be worse off because of it. There are ways to develop trauma resilience which is especially helpful when in a career that will expose you to more traumatic situations. Some signs of traumatic injury are shown below:

Intrusive
- Recurring memories, flashbacks
- Distressing dreams, nightmares
- Re-experience when something reminds you of the event

Avoidance
- Avoiding thoughts, feelings, or physical sensations that reminds of the event
- Avoiding people, situations, places, conversations, activities, or objects

Adaptation
- Unable to remember details of the event
- Developing negative view of yourself or others
- Exaggerated blame of yourself or others

Reactivity
- Become irritable or have outbursts
- Being easily startled
- Being hypervigilant
- Risky behavior
- Trouble sleeping

Fast to Respond

Having the ability to quickly notice negative effects from experiencing trauma is the key to responding. After all, it is difficult to know how to respond if you aren't aware you should respond in the first place.

Learning about the signs and symptoms time means that you have a general awareness of what to look for.

For the next step, let's say you do notice some signs (in yourself or someone else) ... now what?

It is **important not to ignore these signs** as untreated PTSI can contribute to:

- Depression and anxiety
- ncreased use of alcohol or drugs
- Eating and sleep issues
- Suicidal thoughts and actions

If you have experienced a potentially traumatic situation, here are ways to **take early action**:

- **Debrief –** If it was a situation that was part of your work, consider doing a debrief on it. If it's not provided for you, you can use the digital debriefing tool in the HART page in the Driven Resilience App
- **Talk –** Talking with people who care about you and telling them what happened is a very helpful way to start working through it. Even if it hurts to talk, still talk about it – this helps de-power the emotions over time
- **Find help –** Similar to how it's difficult to fix your own arm if you broke the bone, it's also much better to find professional help quickly. If you notice the signs and symptoms, get help soon as it will help you heal faster

A tough part about trauma is the tendency towards **avoidance**. Let's explore this more next.

Overcoming Avoidance

Most people that experience traumatic events eventually overcome it and move on, growing from the experience. However, this is not always the case.

EXAMPLE

Avoiding the Sunset

The thought of working through trauma might be very difficult, but if not dealt with, the effects can cause significant impairment.

For example, if Sandy never deals with the trauma she experienced rock-climbing, then her habit of avoiding sunsets (as one small example) might start to severely influence her life.

The time window of what she considers to be a sunset might expand, resulting in her not wanting to be outside at all anymore, meaning she doesn't want to go to work anymore. She might give up her job and become a shut-in, affecting her relationships with everyone else.

This is a difficult yet important part about dealing with these experiences – we must face our fears. If not, we face a vicious cycle:

- Avoidance leads to short-term relief
- However, this leads to losing confidence in the ability to cope, causing more worrying and more fear
- Leading to greater feelings of anxiety and fear
- Leading to **more avoidance in the future**

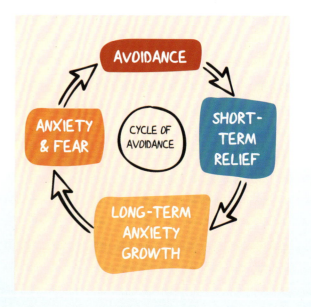

Sunset Exposure

One method to overcome avoidance which is often used is gradual exposure. This is when you are slowly exposed to a stressor to start working through the feelings and behaviors that arise, helping to de-power the stressor.

For example, while Sandy is all shut in avoiding sunsets, she can start to expose herself to it by slowly opening the blinds a little more each day so she can see a bit of the sunset on the floor.

When she feels her heart racing and fear rising, she could use slow breathing to calm the limbic brain, and mindfulness to notice it, not judge it, and let the feeling pass. It might be very hard for her initially, but by continually trying she can keep making progress until eventually she can look again at the sunset without feeling that fear.

Within the brain, this process is about using the prefrontal cortex to de-power the connections that the limbic brain made. She's essentially training her brain again to learn that sunsets aren't dangerous, and the brain doesn't need to worry about them.

Techniques to Develop Trauma Resilience

Apart from responding to the effects of trauma, there are things you can do to harden your mind and resist the effects from taking hold in the first place.

Through training, we can train the **limbic brain to be less reactive,** and in turn **give the prefrontal cortex more control**, allowing you to be more effective in a crisis and experience fewer mental impacts afterwards.

TRAUMA **RESILIENCE**

PRACTICE BUILDS NEURAL CONNECTIONS THAT REDUCE LIMBIC BRAIN ACTIVATION

PFC HAS MORE CONTROL

LIMBIC BRAIN LESS ACTIVE

Captured in War

During a traumatic event, the limbic brain activates strongly when it senses that some of our core needs as humans are being attacked.

This is very relevant in an extreme event such as soldiers being captured in war. Here's how the core needs are affected:

- Sense of **safety** – thoughts like *"I'm going to die"*
- Sense of **control** – thoughts like *"I'm powerless"*
- Sense of **self** – thoughts like *"I'm worthless"*

It's easy to see here how these thoughts contribute to a traumatic experience that can take a long time to overcome.

From the perspective of the brain, if we can train the limbic brain to activate **less strongly** during traumatic situations, then that relative 'calmness' means the chance of a biological injury of PTSI is reduced. Going back to the analogy, instead of breaking a bone, you might just sustain a sprain which heals much faster.

In a way, if you can **find some way to maintain your sense of safety, control, and self** during a traumatic situation, then the effect of that situation will be greatly reduced.

Let's look at techniques that will help to prepare the brain and develop trauma resilience:

- **Pre-exposure**
- **Accept the possibilities**
- **Clarify your language**
- **Get mental insurance**
- **Build general resilience**

ACTIVITY 6.1.9

Take notes on strategies you are using or can use.

Pre-exposure

A way to reduce limbic brain reactivity is through pre-exposure to a controlled version of trauma. Take the example soldiers who might be captured. A situation like that can be traumatic if not prepared for.

However, most armies have a program like the US Survival, Evasion, Resistance, and Escape (SERE) training that prepares soldiers for those situations. This training reduces the activation of the limbic brain by effectively changing beliefs about each core need:

- **Improved** sense of **safety** – thoughts like *"My training will help me survive"*
- **Improved** sense of **control** – thoughts like *"I control how I react"*
- **Improved** sense of **self** – thoughts like *"I'll return with honor"*

  See how much more powerful those statements are?

That kind of thinking in the heat of the moment gives you strength and resilience in the face of a potentially traumatic experience. It will still be tough experience, but you're in a far better position that someone who wasn't prepared.

Pre-exposure

An extension to this is being able to mentally accept the traumatic experiences that you may experience due to your work or even life in general.

Thinking about these events happening might make you feel sad, angry, or depressed. However, full acceptance means no longer feeling that, but instead **you can see the hope for a good life after something traumatic might happen, regardless of how bad it might be at the time it happens.**

Clarify Your Language

The language of trauma in the brain is chaotic. The limbic brain isn't good at making things make sense. It tends to quickly make connections in a fairly inaccurate way to make you remember to avoid similar situations.

To overcome this mess that the limbic brain likes to make, it helps to use the **Concrete Thinking** technique from the HART program. This means thinking through events logically, building a clear timeline and stepping through the details. Practicing this regularly will help keep your mind more organized, even in very difficult situations.

Get Mental Insurance

A great way to make sure you can turn to someone when you need help is **to find a mental health professional now,** even if you don't feel you need one. For people in tough occupations, trauma exposure is a matter of time.

Getting to know someone before you experience trauma is extremely helpful, as they'll have more history about you, know what you were like before it happened, and there to give help much faster. This could be someone like a counsellor, coach, or a close trusted friend. It's basically insurance for you mind.

Build General Resilience

You might have noticed a general theme about all the resilience training we do – just about all of the resilience training is about **maximizing activation of the prefrontal cortex and minimizing limbic brain activation when not needed**.

The more resilient you are in all areas of life, the less vulnerable you are and the more you'll be able to resist the effects of trauma. This means you have strong relationships, strong finances, strong health – constantly investing in yourself helps build an overall confidence that can help protect you.

SCAN ME

Mental Load Management
in the **Driven Resilience App**

Scan the link to access the skill in the app (make sure you are **logged into the app first**).

app.hellodriven.com/activities/1237

TENACITY

6.2

THREE GOOD THINGS

6.2 THREE GOOD THINGS

Learing Outcomes:

- Learn about the way the brain tends to focus on negative events and the consequences of this focus
- Learn about a technique to consciously change the focus of the brain towards positive events
- Practice the Three Good Things technique

This is Useful For:

- Becoming aware of mental filters that might be filtering experiences
- Developing motivation and increasing happiness in tough environments

People in high adversity roles tend to focus mainly on **what was difficult** during the day and ponder things that **went wrong**.

CONSTANT FOCUS ON **WHAT WENT WRONG** CREATES A **MENTAL FILTER**.

After all, when the work you do has high stakes, it's natural to ruminate over difficult events to try and figure out what you could have done better.

There is some value in this to prepare yourself for similar challenges in the future, though it has a downside – **it trains the brain to focus on the negative**.

The Bad, and the Brain

Neural pathways in the brain strengthen the more you use them. This is the basis of how neuroplasticity works - like a muscle, the brain constantly adapts to what it is repeatedly used for.

Soon you have a habit of focusing only on the tough events of the day, and can have a hard time remembering the good things that happened. The brain might not even bother to properly store memories of good things each day, since there's so little mental focus on those events. This constant focus on what went wrong **creates a mental filter**.

This is where a conscious exercise to focus on even just a few good things each day can help to rewire the brain and help improve resilience

SCAN ME

TECHNIQUE

Three Good Things

Scan the code below to use a step-by-step version of the Three Good Things technique in the Driven Resilience App.

PS – make sure you are logged into your app to access this technique.

app.hellodriven.com/activities/791

8   Rippstein-Leuenberger, K., Mauthner, O., Sexton, J. B., & Schwendimann, R. (2017). A qualitative analysis of the Three Good Things intervention in healthcare workers. *BMJ open, 7*(5).

6.2.1 Three Good Things Technique

The task then is quite simple – each day, focus on a few things that went well. These can include many different events:

- It could be something small, like coffee tasting particularly good that day
- It could involve someone else, like a co-worker making a good joke, spending time with someone, and so on
- It could be something big, like getting a job, project, or posting you really wanted
- It could be broad, like simply having had an overall 'good day'

Essentially it can be anything that made you feel happy or positive during the day.

The technique isn't complicated, but there is some brain science involved that results in meaningful impact.

- In fact: People who did this **technique 14 days in a row reported lower symptoms of depression and being happier even after 6 months**[8].
- As you practice this technique your brain will start to hunt each day for good things, and **you'll start noticing more good things in general**

As you get better at recognizing these events, your brain will memorize them better. You may become more attentive, knowing you might want to write down the details later, so you'll want to remember everything. This is how you start to remove the mental filter that tends to focus only on difficult events during the day.

Notes for Effectiveness

Knowing that you should do something is good, but knowing why is useful. Why? It helps to make it clear what the importance of something is, so that you are more likely to stick with it in the long term.

To that effect, here are few important notes about this technique:

- **You must write your answers –** Writing answers (or typing), increases the activation of the areas in your brain we want to activate
- **Nip negativity –** As you write your answers, if you notice you start to get negative, take a moment and refocus on the positive side
- **Do this every day for a few days –** The brain doesn't change after doing this once. Do this for at least five days and consider making this a daily habit for a few weeks

ACTIVITY 6.2.1

When you think about work, what do you mainly think about?

....
....
....
....
....
....
....
....
....
....
....
....
....
....

- **Bonus points if you talk about it –** Telling other people about the good things that happened can help to enhance the effect even further, so tell family, a partner, and friends
- **Write down three good things –** Why three? Usually the first one is easy, the second a bit harder, and by the third one it can be a struggle. And when you start struggling, that's when the brain really starts to adapt and starts noticing more things the next day, because it doesn't want to have to struggle like that again

This technique has been successfully tested with first responders, where it's especially important to take the time to remember good things. Given how easily we can focus on crises and other harsh realities in high adversity work, we need to make an effort beyond most other people to notice the good things in life.

6.2.2 Practice Three Good Things

ACTIVITY 6.2.2

Try out the technique now and think of three good things.

THREE GOOD THINGS

1. What **good thing** happened today?
2. What **caused** this good thing to happen?
3. How did it **make you feel** then, and now as you remember it?

x3

First Good Thing:

What good thing happened today?

....

....

....

....

What caused this good thing to happen?

....

....

....

....

How did it make you feel then, and now as you remember it?

....

....

....

....

Second Good Thing:

What good thing happened today?

....

....

....

....

What caused this good thing to happen?

....

....

....

....

How did it make you feel then, and now as you remember it?

....

....

....

Third Good Thing:

What good thing happened today?

....

....

....

What caused this good thing to happen?

....

....

....

....

How did it make you feel then, and now as you remember it?

....

....

....

SCAN ME

Three Good Things in the Driven Resilience App

Scan the link to access the skill in the app (make sure you are **logged into the app** first).

app.hellodriven.com/activities/1238

NOTES

COLLABORATION

7.1

HIGH QUALITY CONNECTIONS

7.1 HIGH QUALITY CONNECTIONS

Learing Outcomes:

- Learn about the value of high-quality connections
- Learn about the components of quality connections
- Discuss each component and identify actions to build stronger team connections

This is Useful For:

- Building stronger connections with team members
- Building a supportive team environment reduce the impact of these challenges

High adversity work means you need to have better resilience skills than the average person. A key part of resilience is strong relationships with at least a few people – a partner, colleagues, or friends who can help you stay on track and maintain effectiveness.

7.1.1 The Components of Connection

A study conducted over 80 years found that **meaningful relationships are the best predictor of a high quality of life**[9]. For high adversity occupations, this is even more relevant.

Often a major source of strength is the people you work with – the people who experience the same challenges you do. This skill explored different aspects of building high quality connections with those you work with.

This is important to have a sense of trust and safety with your team. This leads to better communication and helps the team improve faster together and work together in time sensitive moments, as well as through training and other times. Not only does that translate to a more **enjoyable working environment**, but it also means **better outcomes in your work**.

SCAN ME

QUICK TEST

Co-worker Connection Quality Check

Scan the code below to complete a short assessment of your current experience with co-workers. You can do this assessment again later to see how your skill changes over time. PS – make sure you are logged into your app to access this assessment.this assessment.

app.hellodriven.com/activities/854

9   Waldinger, R., & Schulz, M. (2023). *The Good Life: Lessons from the World's Longest Scientific Study of Happiness.* Simon and Schuster.

Building Quality Connections

Great connections come from a combination of three factors – **cognitions**, **emotions**, and **behaviors**.

Cognitions refer to how your mind (and the minds of others) works. Cognitions and mental processes inform emotions and behaviors. These include:

- Awareness of others
- Impressions of others
- Taking perspective

Emotions are your own emotional reactions to people and work, along with understanding the emotional reactions of others. These include:

- Constructive emotions
- Emotional contagion
- Empathy

Behaviors are the physical actions you and others exhibit in the work environment. These form from awareness and emotional reaction, and include:

- Respect
- Enabling tasks
- Play and games

Connection is not about one simple thing – it's a combination of these three factors. As we go through each one, you'll see how they work together to form meaningful connections that foster a strong culture.

The combination of these building blocks creates high quality connections which look like this:

People show **genuine interest in each other**

- They **offer help and assist** each other, contributing to more effectiveness on jobs and calls
- They inject positivity to make high adversity work more enjoyable and rewarding
- They **uncover common ground** to build relationships, even with minimal time available and through exhaustion

Now we can delve deeper into each factor and find ways you can use these to better understand others and form stronger connections.

NOTES

ACTIVITY 7.1.1

Thinking about those four points above (showing interest, offer help, inject positivity, common ground), what's working and what could be better?

....
....
....
....
....
....
....
....
....
....
....
....
....
....
....
....
....
....
....

7.1.2 Exploring Cognitions

Cognitions are about how your mind works, as well as the minds of others. This means that apart from having a good awareness of your own mind, you should also have:

- Strong awareness of others
- Be aware of your impressions of others
- And have the ability to take perspective

Do you sometimes…

- Forget there are other people around you?
- Lose touch about what the goals are of others?
- Forget details about people or what they do?

What does it feel like when it happens to you?

....
....
....
....
....
....
....
....
....
....
....
....
....
....

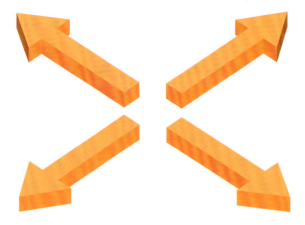

Awareness of Others

The first step to connection is being aware of people around you. This means maintaining a relative degree of **situational awareness** when you're around co-workers. This includes:

▲ **Realizing** there are people around you. It's easy to get so focused on a task that you forget about those nearby and don't acknowledge their presence

▲ **Understanding** the behaviors and goals of people around you. This helps to make sure your goals align, and offering help at appropriate times

▲ **Being able to recognize** and recall details about people (for example, John likes vanilla ice cream) and what they tend to do (John looks after that specific equipment)

▲ **Being aware** of different cognitions, emotions, and behaviors between you and other people

As the title suggests, it's mainly about awareness. Maintaining this awareness of others through simple communication can already help to build relationships.

ACTIVITY 7.1.2

Which ideas can you use to be more mindful of your impressions of others?

Ideas to Improve Impressions

Though here are some challenges you might face, and ideas to consider:

☐ When you're exhausted from long hours and tough work, it can be hard to maintain awareness of others. Although it's tough, make an effort to **acknowledge those around you** – even if it's to say "Man, I'm wiped out!" so they know not to expect deep conversations

☐ Being physically separated makes awareness hard. For this, make a point to **check in with people** and ask what they're up to and how they're doing

☐ If you've just faced something difficult it can be easy to retreat into yourself. At these times try to **make a simple connection** like saying "Hey, that was tough" – especially if there was someone else that experienced it with you

ACTIVITY 7.1.3

Which ideas can you use to be more mindful of your impressions of others?

Ideas to Improve Impressions

A way to reduce limbic brain reactivity is through pre-exposure to a controlled version of trauma. Take the example soldiers who might be captured. A situation like that can be traumatic if not prepared for.

☐ Realize that you might **meet co-workers at difficult times**. This means your initial impression of them has a higher likelihood of not being accurate. In high adversity work, be prepared to give people more time to make an impression, and give them the benefit of the doubt during that time

☐ When **working with the public** know that you likely are meeting them at difficult times as well. Reserve judgement on them, knowing that their behavior is not typical of their daily manner

☐ Be aware of **the impression you make** with others. If you tend to be short with people, tend to be stand-offish, not smile when you meet people, and so on, then people will assume you would rather not connect. Trying to be open and show friendliness helps to build quality connections

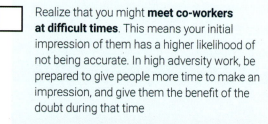

Impressions of Others

We often make rapid judgements of others based on initial impressions of something they do or say.

Here are a couple of examples:

▲ Many of our impressions are based on **non-verbal cues**, like tone of voice, gestures, and facial expressions

▲ Impressions might be about someone's warmth, friendliness, acceptance, and so on. This gives you an idea **how interested they might be** to connect again in future, and potential for a higher quality connection

▲ **Posture and behavior** impressions can suggest if someone is open to chat, or if

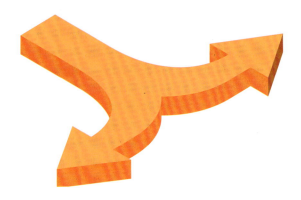

Taking Perspective

Having a balanced impression of people is important, and the next big step is **seeing the world through someone else's eyes**. This is because:

- Being willing to take someone else's perspective means having the **courage to admit** that it's ok for someone else to have a different perspective from you
- This facilitates compassion (**empathy plus the intention to help**) to support others in achieving their goals, even if they may be different from yours
- It helps you **predict the behaviors** of others, as you don't expect them to behave as you would, but you expect them to behave as they would

 **ACTIVITY 7.1.4**

Which ideas can you use to improve how you take perspective of others?

Ideas to Improve Perspective Taking

Here's how you can incorporate more of this:

Being willing to **adapt your behavior** to the people you work with can help show that you care about them, fostering a deeper connection. Look for ways in which you can get your work done while also supporting their goals

Taking the time to talk to your co-workers about **how they would handle situations** can enhance effectiveness on calls as you know each other better and can avoid mistakes while working faster

Taking perspective is a further step to learn about someone and build an internal model of them in your mind so that you can better predict their behavior. This deeper connection and understanding helps improve mutual performance.

 **ACTIVITY 7.1.5**

Which ideas can you use to improve the emotions you take to work?

Ideas to Explore Emotions

Some challenges and tips to think about:

☐ It can be hard to show positive emotions when you're tired or in a rush. Even if you're rushing from one job to the next, still push yourself to **show gratitude for someone else's help**. That small moment can help build life-long relationships

☐ When someone did something well, make a point to **recognize good work**

☐ Whenever someone puts effort into a task, or maybe even did something that wasn't necessarily their job, let them know you **appreciate the effort**

☐ Given your line of work it can be more common for people to express negative emotions. Use this knowledge to **understand why someone might be in a bad mood** – don't judge them for it, and don't take it personally

☐ In really difficult situations **use the Reappraisal technique** to shift your mood towards something more constructive

◢ ....

◢ ....

◢ ....

◢ ....

◢ ....

◢ ....

◢ ....

◢ ....

◢ ....

◢ ....

7.1.3 Exploring Emotions

Emotions come from beliefs and cognitions. How we guide our own emotions and interpret those of others affects how likely we are to connect, and the quality of connections. As you'll see, some of these also influence the likelihood that others would want to connect with you. Emotions include:

◢ Constructive emotions

◢ Emotional contagion

◢ Empathy

Let's start with a familiar concept.

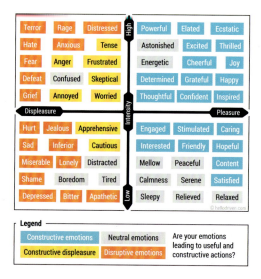

Constructive Emotions

In the Reappraisal technique we talked about the concept of **constructive emotions** which are generally emotions that help us achieve our goals and feel good about ourselves.

These are emotions such as determination, gratitude, excitement, hope, and so on. The mood chart is also included at the end of this manual if you'd like to explore it further.

Let's explore these aspects. In particular:

◢ Constructive emotions help people **get through difficult tasks** and share those good feelings with others helps to build relationships

◢ It's not about always being happy – that's not natural. It's normal to be sad or angry sometimes. It's more about **your general disposition**. If you're sad all the time, then it's something to investigate

◢ Constructive emotions **activate the prefrontal cortex**. This improves resourcefulness, problem-solving, and strategic thinking. All of these are important for your work

ACTIVITY 7.1.6

Which ideas can you use to employ emotional contagion as a way to build connection?

Ideas to Influence Contagion

Knowing this about emotional contagion, there are some things to consider:

☐ When your co-workers have been through a tough challenge, keep in mind the emotional contagion effect to notice **if a negative mood is taking over** the group

☐ You can also use the contagion effect to facilitate higher moods in the group during good times. Sometimes one person's refusal to share in a group mood (like celebration or sharing a joke) can bring everyone down. Where appropriate, **join in group** moods to help the team build stronger connections together

☐ Having noticed negative emotional contagion, you can use Reappraisal to **consciously shift the mood of the group**. Here the main challenge is to find the appropriate emotion to shift to – refer to the chart to help make a match whether it may be determination, or gratitude, this will help to overcome a disruptive mindset in the group

Emotional Contagion

An interesting aspect of emotions is that they tend to spread.

- ◢ The human brain has **mirror neurons** that automatically help us to feel the emotions of others through facial expressions, gestures, and tone of voice
- ◢ This leads to **unconscious mirroring** of each other's voice patterns and behaviors, helping to build an emotional connection between people
- ◢ One person's emotions can **influence a group**, either unintentionally, or intentionally

YOU INFLUENCE OTHERS. USE THAT INFLUENCE TO BUILD A **STRONG TEAM.**

ACTIVITY 7.1.7

Which ideas can you use to help manage empathy in your work?

Ideas to Manage Empathy

Here are four ideas:

☐ A challenge could be that you reduce your own emotional reactions to reduce the impact of the work you do. Over time this could make it harder to empathize with co-workers and other people. After all, if something doesn't bother you, you might assume it doesn't bother them either. This assumption can be wrong, so try to **purposefully dial empathy** based on the situation

☐ Remember the lessons from carer satisfaction, where too much empathy can lead to compassion fatigue. Where necessary, keep a level of professional detachment

☐ Note as well that purposefully removing empathy can also lead to becoming cynical or coming across as cold. **Find a healthy balance**

☐ Something that's often overlooked is to also **have empathy for yourself**. Sometimes emotions can be pushed aside since you don't have time to deal with them, but they don't go away. Allow yourself time to process emotional events. Know that it's ok for some situations to affect you – it means you are still human

◢ ....

◢ ....

◢ ....

◢ ....

◢ ....

◢ ....

◢ ....

◢ ....

◢ ....

Empathy

Empathy – the ability to understand and feel someone else's emotions – is a key part of building quality relationships.

◢ The ability to **understand and feel** someone else's emotions

◢ Empathy leads towards **warmth, caring and compassion** (the desire to help and support someone)

◢ This **builds on awareness and taking perspective** to help predict how someone would feel in particular situations (for example "Sally would appreciate this" or "Mark is probably struggling right now")

◢ Showing empathy is a **key emotional intelligence skill**, leading to others liking you and enjoying your presence

7.1.4 Exploring Behaviors

The useful thing about behaviors is that they are **easier to observe and notice**. While cognitions and emotions are the foundation, behaviors are mostly what people experience about you and how you learn about them. As the saying goes, actions speak louder than words, and much louder than thoughts, so to speak.

Behaviors include:

- Respect
- Enabling tasks
- Play and games

Respect

Respect is an important part of human relationships. Respecting others starts with respecting yourself. From there you can work on showing it:

- **Respect is mostly shown in non-verbal ways.** This includes turning towards someone when they speak to you, making eye contact, acknowledging what people say, and taking what they say seriously

- **Respect is also about verbal cues,** such as using an appropriate tone of voice and language appropriate for the situation

- It's also about **what you do**, including following through on commitments you make and keeping in mind what consequences your actions might have on them down the road

- Showing respect lets people feel they are being **treated with dignity**, which increases their desire to want to connect with you further

 **ACTIVITY 7.1.8**

Which ideas can you use to employ emotional contagion as a way to build connection?

Ideas to Manage Empathy

Here are some ways to observe how you are showing respect to those in and around your work:

☐ At all levels in your work, **respect can be a useful ally to build connections.** If you're new, it can help to show **respect for the veterans** – respect their experience and knowledge and take opportunities to learn from them. If you're a veteran, **respect the newbies** and take time to teach them so they learn faster

☐ Even when dealing with members of the public, keep in mind how showing **respect can lead to better outcome**s – for example, more cooperation, putting people at ease, less irrational action

☐ In these types of work environments, it can be part of the culture to heckle and prank people. Sometimes it can all be in good fun, though it easily becomes disrespectful, or worse. **Keep in mind where the line is between fun and disrespect**

⊿ ....

⊿ ....

⊿ ....

⊿ ....

⊿ ....

⊿ ....

⊿ ....

⊿ ....

⊿ ....

ACTIVITY 7.1.9

Which ideas can you use to improve how you enable tasks?

Ideas Around Enabling Tasks

A few things for you to look out for:

☐ Some routine tasks can be tedious and draining. Joining in to help a co-worker complete these tasks while also **injecting some positivity** can help make these tasks fun and also build better connections

☐ When you're in a rush/in your zone you can trample over what other people are doing and not realize how you're impacting them. Even in major crises, still aim to maintain higher **situational awareness** to notice if you're about to accidentally interfere with someone else

....
....
....
....
....
....
....
....
....
....
....
....
....
....
....
....

Enabling Tasks

Practical assistance and helping those around you get their work done is a great way to build relationships with co-workers. This includes:

▴ Physically helping someone to get their work done

▴ Show you are willing to put in your own time and effort to help them succeed, **showing support, empathy,** and awareness of where they may need help

▴ Sometimes it's about **not standing in the way** of someone else doing their work. It's possible that you may be unintentionally preventing someone else from doing their work due to something you're working on. Being mindful of this and shifting things around so it can work for both of you can help demonstrate awareness and respect

▴ While helping is good, take care to not undermine someone's **self-efficacy and learning**. Always doing things for someone can leave them feeling inadequate. There is the line to find between helping when they need it, and letting them learn and help themselves when useful

Play and Games

The last component is about just **having some fun at work**. It doesn't always have to be super serious and focused. Sharing lighter moments at work is an important part of connection and flows to outside of work.

- ▵ Traditions, mascots, team games – these can all help form a culture where work is also **mixed with humor and enjoyment**
- ▵ Adding play and humor also helps to add some variety to what would otherwise be very similar days
- ▵ This helps to **reduce stress and break tension**, especially during tough situations. Embracing these opportunities and joining in play with the team is a useful way to enable positive emotional contagion
- ▵ Relaxing through play **helps people open up** and learn about each other. This can extend to after-hours socializing to build much deeper and lasting friendship

ACTIVITY 7.1.10

Which ideas can you try to incorporate play and games?

Ideas for Play and Games

Here are a couple of things to keep in mind with your work:

☐ Working long hours and shifts can leave little time to get to know co-workers. Maybe after all that you just want to get home and don't have energy left for socializing. However, try to still join in as **socializing can help boost energy in the future.** It can make the work environment more enjoyable when it includes stronger relationships

☐ Keep in mind that relaxing, making jokes, and using humor doesn't mean you don't take the job seriously. In fact, these are **important coping skills** for making high adversity work sustainable. But do keep an awareness of what is appropriate, so you don't overstep the bounds

....
....
....
....
....
....
....
....
....
....
....
....
....

ACTIVITY 7.1.11

Look back – what are your top actions to build more high-quality connections?

....
....
....
....
....
....
....
....
....
....
....
....
....
....
....
....
....
....
....
....

The challenge is in keeping these concepts in the back of your mind so that you can use them as appropriate **and build on them over time.**

No one is born with great social skills. It all takes practice and effort over time. Naturally, building these skills here also translates into improved relationships with friends,

COLLABORATION

7.2

GRIEF & GROWTH

7.2 GRIEF & GROWTH

Everyone experiences loss through life. It could be losing something or someone due to death or breakup of a relationship. **Working in a high adversity occupation means you will be more exposed to this than most people.**

Learning how to deal with grief – both your own and that of others, **is an important skill to develop**.

Let's first understand the process of grief more, then we can look at some specific examples that you might have to deal with at some point.

7.2.1   Two Processes of Grief

There used to be a view that grief progressed through five stages: denial, anger, bargaining, depression, and acceptance.

Our understanding has now improved, and we recognize that the five stages don't really represent how it works for everyone. In fact, **each person's experience of grief is unique** and there's **no standard answer for how grief should proceed**.

Some emotions that may come up include:

- Shock & disbelief
- Numbness
- Intense pain and sadness
- Guilt and regret
- Anger and resentment
- Loneliness and abandonment

For many people there are **two types of processes** that they deal with after the initial shock and pain or numbness of loss.

- **Grieving –** This includes coping with the pain of memories, longing, thinking about the person – basically the most painful parts:
- **Adapting –** Often we also need to cope with having to adapt to a changed life due to the loss. Such as having to do tasks that the person used to do or adapting routines:

At the same time, these don't usually take up all your time when grieving. There are also other things in life that keep on going, like still having to pay bills, going to work, doing chores and so on.

Let's explore the two processes and see how they work together.

Grieving

This is where you are mainly focused on aspects directly related to the loss. Consider:

- Thinking about the person that is gone (such as a breakup) or has passed away
- Memories about what life used to be like with them
- Longing to be with them
- Going through old photos
- Wondering how they might have reacted to something
- Realizing old bonds have now been broken and accepting that

Some of these may involve good feelings, others may be painful. In the beginning it's mostly painful, though over time you are likely to have more positive feelings about these memories, turning into a kind of nostalgia.

Here it's helpful to talk to people about it, talk about the hard parts, feel the emotions that come with them and allow yourself to be sad and grieve as a natural part of working through the pain.

Adapting

In a way, losing someone also results in the loss of other things.

Like having a partner that used to help maintain the house, do the finances, do cooking, give advice, enjoy activities with, etc.

Losing someone means also losing that contribution to your life, meaning a **secondary loss** that adds to the pain of simply losing someone you loved.

This is where part of grieving is about adapting to how life has changed after loss, including:

- Changing routines & adapting tasks
- Taking on new responsibilities
- Building new relationships
- Doing new activities
- Distractions from grief
- Avoidance of pain and denial

You can see how adapting can quickly mix with grief, where having to do something that someone else used to do could result in longing and missing that person. That's natural.

While going through your daily life you would likely have moments of grieving, moments of working through adaptation, as well as dealing with all the normal life stuff that needs to be done.

NOTES

ACTIVITY 7.2.1

What are your thoughts on this model of grief?
What is your view on grieving & adapting?

◣...

◣...

◣...

◣...

◣...

◣...

◣...

◣...

◣...

◣...

◣...

◣...

Avoidance is... Normal?

Interestingly, some level of avoidance is a natural part of the grieving process (as long as this is not done excessively).

After all, losing someone close to you doesn't mean you have to be sad 100% of the time for a while.

For example, avoiding the pain through distractions can be helpful, such as:

⬓ Keeping yourself busy with work tasks

⬓ Cooking and preparing meals

⬓ Talking with friends about unrelated topics

⬓ Watching a movie

⬓ Exercising and being active

⬓ Engaging in other hobbies

The point of activities like these is not to fully avoid every feeling of loss, but rather to provide a mental break from sadness. They also help to remind you that life goes on and you can enjoy life again, even if it is different than before.

In this way, avoidance is a natural part of working through grief. Importantly, this doesn't mean you should constantly suppress emotions – this can be harmful in itself.

This is where you'll find oscillation – jumping between periods of mourning and periods of distraction. Over time, what generally happens is that the periods of sadness become shorter and more infrequent, and you become more engaged in your new adapted life.

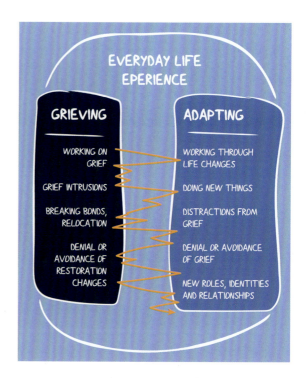

7.2.2 Pre-Acceptance & Your Brain

Loss affects us severely when we're very unprepared for it and its consequences. This is where a very strong reaction from the limbic brain can create a **highly emotionally charged memory** from that news of the loss.

Especially if the brain is unprepared or is very worried about a potential loss (such as for a partner that has a dangerous job).

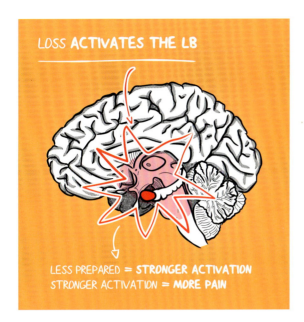

LOSS **ACTIVATES THE LB**

LESS PREPARED = **STRONGER ACTIVATION**
STRONGER ACTIVATION = **MORE PAIN**

Therefore, practicing some form of **acceptance prior to loss** can help to reduce the effect. This is through reducing the level of activation of the limbic brain, mainly because you've already thought about it and started to think about **constructive ways of managing a potential loss in the future.**

In fact, this is an ancient practice for many. For example:

- **Buddhists** practice a concept called non-attachment. After all, it's our desire to remain attached to things and people that cause us to feel loss
- **Stoicism** practices not being affected by desire, or fear, or pain, and instead uses logic to understand the world and accept the moment as it is

That's not to say these methods are necessarily the answer, but they certainly provide an idea of what helps to reduce grief in the future.

A practical method to do this is to accept the possibility of different situations happening ahead of time.

There are some realities in the world of responders that are more common than other occupations.

These include:

- Supporting/dealing with someone else's grieving
- Death of someone close
- Suicide of someone at work
- Suicide of someone close

These are difficult topics, though since they are very much a reality in the world of responders, it's important to think through these more to prepare your mind so you are better able to deal with the impact if or when they occur.

EXAMPLE

A Note on Focus

It's important not to become too focused on negative future events to the point that you are endlessly worrying about future scenarios.

The goal is to **think constructively** about what might happen – what can you do to be proactive and think about how you can still live a full life even if something did happen.

ACTIVITY 7.2.2

Given the challenges you might face in your work, have you done some type of pre-acceptance?

....
....
....
....
....
....
....
....
....
....
....
....
....
....
....
....

7.2.3 Supporting Someone Who's Grieving

A situation you might face is when someone else has experienced a loss and you are around to support them.

These could be colleagues, members of the public, family, or friends. There may be breakups, people moving away or out of the house, the loss of a loved one, a suicide, a life changing injury or diagnosis, loss of possessions, and so on.

These times can be hard since they are incredibly emotional. Sometimes you might feel their pain intensely, or you may be unsure how to handle the situation. It can also be complex when you know they need support, but perhaps you have limited time as there are other people that also need your help.

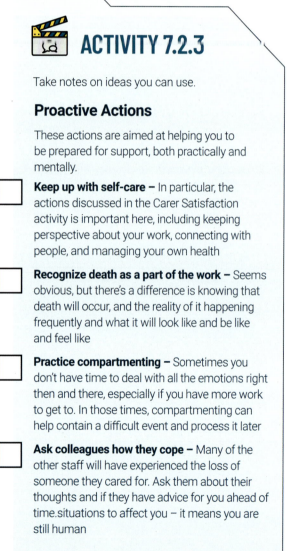

ACTIVITY 7.2.3

Take notes on ideas you can use.

Proactive Actions

These actions are aimed at helping you to be prepared for support, both practically and mentally.

☐ **Keep up with self-care** – In particular, the actions discussed in the Carer Satisfaction activity is important here, including keeping perspective about your work, connecting with people, and managing your own health

☐ **Recognize death as a part of the work** – Seems obvious, but there's a difference is knowing that death will occur, and the reality of it happening frequently and what it will look like and be like and feel like

☐ **Practice compartmenting** – Sometimes you don't have time to deal with all the emotions right then and there, especially if you have more work to get to. In those times, compartmenting can help contain a difficult event and process it later

☐ **Ask colleagues how they cope** – Many of the other staff will have experienced the loss of someone they cared for. Ask them about their thoughts and if they have advice for you ahead of time.situations to affect you – it means you are still human

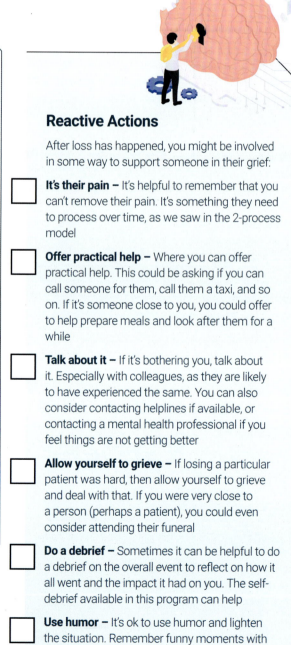

Reactive Actions

After loss has happened, you might be involved in some way to support someone in their grief:

☐ **It's their pain** – It's helpful to remember that you can't remove their pain. It's something they need to process over time, as we saw in the 2-process model

☐ **Offer practical help** – Where you can offer practical help. This could be asking if you can call someone for them, call them a taxi, and so on. If it's someone close to you, you could offer to help prepare meals and look after them for a while

☐ **Talk about it** – If it's bothering you, talk about it. Especially with colleagues, as they are likely to have experienced the same. You can also consider contacting helplines if available, or contacting a mental health professional if you feel things are not getting better

☐ **Allow yourself to grieve** – If losing a particular patient was hard, then allow yourself to grieve and deal with that. If you were very close to a person (perhaps a patient), you could even consider attending their funeral

☐ **Do a debrief** – Sometimes it can be helpful to do a debrief on the overall event to reflect on how it all went and the impact it had on you. The self-debrief available in this program can help

☐ **Use humor** – It's ok to use humor and lighten the situation. Remember funny moments with the pat

Ideas for Supporting Others

If your organization provides specific training for these events, follow those protocols. Otherwise, here are some more ideas on what to say and what not to say to someone grieving:

Things to Say

Things NOT to Say

Which of these ideas could you use more when supporting others who are grieving?

....

....

....

....

....

....

....

....

....

....

TECHNIQUE

Talk Through Grief

Scan the code below to use a step-by-step activity to talk through grief in the Driven Resilience App. Note, this activity specifically applies to when you have experienced loss.

PS – make sure you are logged into your app to access this technique.

app.hellodriven.com/activities/864

NOTES

....

....

....

....

....

....

....

....

....

....

....

....

7.2.4 Death of Someone Close

There are all kinds of ways these challenges appear in our lives.

- Sometimes it may be sudden due to an accident or incident at work
- Sometimes it can be gradual, like a fight with cancer or another disease
- Sometimes it may be complicated, like someone in a coma where you're not quite sure how you should be feeling

Reactions to this are basically what we mentioned last time, having to deal with the emotions that come up as part of grieving, as well as having to adapt to a new life where things are now different from before.

Sometimes we might feel like we couldn't live without someone. Then when they die, we must face the reality that we now actually have to go on.

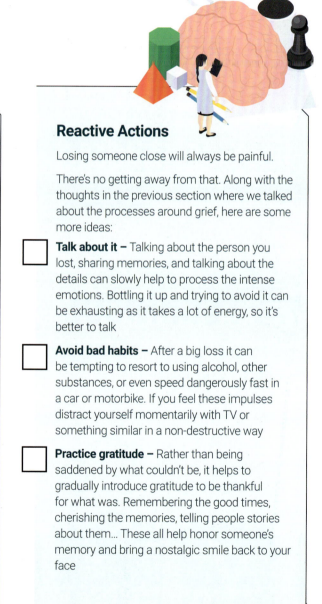

Proactive Actions

The way you live now affects how you experience loss later. Here are some ideas to build resilience around grief.

☐ **Appreciate people now –** So often we only recognize what we had after loss. Even things like little arguments become cherished memories. With that in mind, make a conscious effort to appreciate people while they are alive right now. Doing so means you'll have less regrets later

☐ **Broaden your network –** If you're highly dependent on one person, then their loss will be much more intense than if you had a broader network that you can rely on. For example, invest in friendships and build more connections with family members

☐ **Have a resilient purpose –** Loss is very intense if your identity and purpose is wrapped around someone else. Such as if your purpose in life is to "Be a good dad", then losing a child is devastating on multiple fronts since you not only lose a child but also lose your identity and purpose at the same time. Having a more resilient purpose such as "Help people", of which your child is one person you help, then loss doesn't take away your identity and purpose. It will still be devastating, but you'll have more reason to keep on going

Reactive Actions

Losing someone close will always be painful.

There's no getting away from that. Along with the thoughts in the previous section where we talked about the processes around grief, here are some more ideas:

☐ **Talk about it –** Talking about the person you lost, sharing memories, and talking about the details can slowly help to process the intense emotions. Bottling it up and trying to avoid it can be exhausting as it takes a lot of energy, so it's better to talk

☐ **Avoid bad habits –** After a big loss it can be tempting to resort to using alcohol, other substances, or even speed dangerously fast in a car or motorbike. If you feel these impulses distract yourself momentarily with TV or something similar in a non-destructive way

☐ **Practice gratitude –** Rather than being saddened by what couldn't be, it helps to gradually introduce gratitude to be thankful for what was. Remembering the good times, cherishing the memories, telling people stories about them... These all help honor someone's memory and bring a nostalgic smile back to your face

7.2.5 Loss Due to Suicide

This is one of the hardest things to deal with – the suicide of someone close like a friend, family member, a partner, or even a child.

Powerful emotions follow, such as extreme shock, disbelief, anger, guilt, confusion, abandonment, and despair.

Along with sadness, feelings of guilt might emerge, such as:

- *"If only I knew..."*
- *"What if I..."*
- *"I wish I..."*

And so on, causing a lot of rumination and grieving, making it hard to focus on work in the meantime.

When it's about someone at work, often there is news or gossip about the circumstances contributing to the suicide. For example:

- Dealing with too much stress
- Mounting financial or relationship issues
- Dealing with harassment or abuse
- Not enough support, etc

When it seems like work contributed to suicide, then feelings of anger about the workplace or work culture can emerge.

This is where proactive actions are ideally what we need to invest in, though there are also considerations to keep in mind on the reactive side.

NOTES

Proactive Actions

Here are some ideas to support suicide prevention.

- [ ] **First, support openness –** Building trust and being open with your family, friends, and team members is important for them to be able to talk about their own mental health can help with identifying if there's an issue ahead of time

- [ ] **Recognize it can happen –** Even though the ideal would be that this never happens, and that's what we work towards, the reality is that it still happens. Accepting that this can happen, and especially that it is even more likely in your line of work will make it less of a shock if it happens, and will also help you take prevention more seriously

- [ ] **Look for signs –** Trauma and depression lead to a higher risk of suicide. Take care to understand those signs and symptoms, as they might help you spot someone at risk. Sometimes people may also express deeper truths like these through humor. Though, take care not to blame yourself if something happens regardless of signs

- [ ] **Support programs –** From HART, through to other initiative that can help to reduce suicide risk. And lead by example to show that you take this seriously, you work on your mental fitness, and you encourage everyone around you to do the same

- [ ] **Recognise that life would go on –** This can be a tough one, but being able to recognise ahead of time that if anyone were to end their lives this way, your life would go on. Having your own independent identity and a purpose in your life that's not centred on one person is important, as that will be your continued purpose after an event like this

Reactive Actions

Losing someone close will always be painful. There's no getting away from that. Along with the thoughts in the previous section where we talked about the processes around grief, here are some more ideas:

- [ ] **Take care of yourself –** Sometimes after a loss like this you can fall into deep despair and grief, where you stop looking after yourself. If you are struggling here, ask for help

- [ ] **Avoid *"What if's"* and *"If onlys"* –** These are tempting questions and scenarios, but they are unanswerable and lead to unhelpful rumination - painful thoughts without resolution. Focus on who is still around (including yourself!) and work on building a new life

- [ ] **Avoid spending too long on asking *"Why?"* –** You can spend years asking this question and still don't understand. It can be enough to get a basic understanding of what the situation was, then accept the loss as something tragic and simply allow yourself to grieve

- [ ] **Avoid thinking *"It was my fault"* or *"I could/ should have stopped them"* –** Accept that they made a decision for themselves, and it wasn't your fault. Blaming yourself doesn't change the situation nor brings them back

Focus on the future and on taking constructive action – Specifically if it was the suicide of someone at work that you might not have known personally, use a situation like this as motivation to build a more supportive culture, reducing stigma around mental health and supporting others to heal from the event

- [ ] **Grieve –** If it affects you directly, allow yourself to grieve and go through the pain. Then allow yourself to move on and continue living, eventually enjoying life again

Complicated Grief

Complicated grief is a more technical term for when grief doesn't resolve naturally. For example:

- **Constantly avoiding** the grief and going on as if nothing happened, often resulting in unwanted intrusive memories

- **A constant state of sadness** that's not getting any better, with no periods of distraction or attending to the rest of your life (meaning no oscillation)

- **PTSI symptoms** due to a loss involved with a traumatic experience

- **Feeling depressed** and unable to move on, unable to enjoy life anymore, and seeing no hope of things improving

- **Increased use** of alcohol or substances to cope, or dangerous and risky behavior

If these types of behaviors appear, it is a good sign to reach out to a mental health professional to help work through the loss.

Final Notes

One important action is to **make the most of your time and the people you have** here now. Appreciate the people in your life and everyone around you. Appreciate the time you have on this earth. Don't worry too much about the small stuff, and if you don't like something, either change it or change your situation.

After loss, there is still a world full of people left. Be grateful for whatever you do have still and the people who keep on living.

Even in the darkest depths of grief, you can still find a little bit of light that you can grow into a beacon of hope for yourself and those around you.

NOTES

CHOOSE TO **GROW FROM LOSS** AND AIM YOUR GROWTH TOWARDS **BUILDING A BETTER WORLD.**

ACTIVITY 7.2.4

What can you do proactively? For example:

- ◢ Appreciate people now
- ◢ Build your network
- ◢ Support openness
- ◢ Lead by example

◢ ....

◢ ....

◢ ....

◢ ....

◢ ....

◢ ....

◢ ....

◢ ....

◢ ....

◢ ....

◢ ....

◢ ....

◢ ....

◢ ....

◢ ....

◢ ....

◢ ....

◢ ....

◢ ....

SCAN ME

Grief & Growth in the **Driven Resilience App**

Scan the link to access the skill in the app (make sure you are **logged into the app** first).

app.hellodriven.com/activities/1240

NOTES

COLLABORATION

7.3

STRONG
CONNECTIONS

7.3 STRONG RELATIONSHIPS

Learing Outcomes:

- Learn ways to help manage relational challenges proactively
- Explore a variety of strategies to establish healthy boundaries
- Provides a step-by-step guide in using the active-constructive responding technique

This is Useful For:

- Building a healthy relationship with a partner
- Improving communication skills with people you care about

High adversity work tends to have strong influences on relationships. Skills here are worth learning regardless of if you have a romantic partner, since these skills are important to have if you do develop a relationship in the future.

Additionally, these skills also apply to interacting with friends and family, so let's look at a few key things:

- Understanding relationship challenges
- Returning & leaving home
- Setting boundaries & making time
- Using active constructive responding

7.3.1 Establishing Routines

High adversity work in general comes with challenges for relationships. That's just the reality of the work, for example:

- Being **exhausted** from long hours and having no energy left to talk
- **Work hours** might not work well together, meaning you see very little of your partner
- Having your mind feel fried from **managing crises** all day
- Spending all day dealing with traumatic stuff that you might **not want to bother** your partner with, leaving you little to talk about
- Having to deal personally with traumatic experiences that are **hard to share**
- Potentially getting **called away** for an extended period due to some crisis, adding uncertainty to the relationship
- Having a partner that's worried about your **health and safety** because of the type of work you do

And all kinds of other challenges in-between. In short, these jobs aren't the easiest thing in the world when it comes to maintaining a relationship (or even dating in the first place).

Building personal skills and quite a bit of open communication can help make things a little easier here and keep you and your partner satisfied with the relationship.

SAVE SOME **ENERGY** FOR THE **PEOPLE** THAT **MATTER.**

Returning & Leaving Home

A good place to start is thinking about when you come home and leave for work.

When you've been working long hours spending time managing crises and traumatic situations, coming home at the end of the day can be a challenge by itself.

- When you come home you might simply **not have energy** to chat and would rather just sleep for a full day to recover. You likely have your head full of work stuff and just want to crash when you walk in the door
- At the same time, when you leave for work, it might be at **unusual times** when others are still asleep or not around

However, take a minute to consider – does your work get the best of you, while the people that live with you get the scraps? If these are people you truly care about, do they not perhaps also deserve some of the best of you? And don't you also want that for them too?

This is about setting up a routine to improve the quality of time you get together, as well as setting clear expectations. Doing this helps remind you as well to **save some energy for the people that matter** to you and not spend it all at work.

 **ACTIVITY 7.3.1**

Ideas for Routines

Here are some examples to get you thinking about routines for leaving and returning:

Leaving for Work

Make the most of this time together. Ideally fit in some quality time that's not just a big rush. Here's an example:

- [ ] If possible, **get together for a meal** before you leave. This might involve timing the meal to fit into your schedule

- [ ] Talk about **non-work-related stuff**. Catch up with what's been happening with each other, make plans for things to do together, make jokes, and enjoy the moment

- [ ] When you finally head out, make a point to **hug each other**. Not just a quick hug and peck goodbye, but a proper longer hug that you can let linger for a while – really feel each other's presence

- [ ] And with that, **head out** for a productive day!

Returning Home

If you've been working long hours, this can be challenging. Still, the idea is to bring home a little bit of the best of you for those you care about. For example:

- [ ] On your way home, **think about something positive** from work you can share. If you do a commute, this can be a great time to do the Three Good Things technique and share those things with people at home, or share something interesting you learned

- [ ] When you walk in, gather some energy, and **let people know you are home**

- [ ] **Hug each other again**, and as before, let it linger so you can properly feel each other's presence. Might as well keep hugging for a bit while talking

- [ ] **Avoid offloading** a bunch of bad stuff from work. Share something positive or interesting, and ask people about their day

From there, you can set up a routine about getting rest and recovering from work.

PS – this doesn't mean you need to be positive all the time, but it can help to generally keep those initial moments that you see each other again to be positive. Make your reunion something to look forward to each time. There's always time later to go into deeper stuff if you need to.

Even if you live by yourself, a routine like this can help you separate work from home so you relax & recharge better.

How can you improve your daily routine (before heading out & when returning home) to help your relationship or yourself?

....
....
....
....
....
....
....
....
....
....
....
....
....
....
....

MAKE YOUR REUNION SOMETHING TO LOOK FORWARD TO EACH TIME.

7.3.2 Setting Boundaries & Making Time

How you treat your partner naturally makes a big difference in the quality of the relationship.

Though working in high adversity occupations often means that you identify so strongly with work that it is also where your mind is most of the time, it might be what you talk about most of the time, and it constantly pops up in your home life.

Next, let's explore this more in terms of boundaries, making time, and active constructive responding.

EXAMPLE

Warning Signs

Here are some warning signs for things that might be putting your relationships at home at risk:

- You spend a **long time recovering** from work, leaving very little quality time with family
- Always **giving in to work** demands, meaning you constantly skip on family time or events to work more
- All you **talk about is work** and stories from work, rarely about other parts of life
- You **constantly ask** your partner for advice about stuff from work
- You **are on edge**, easily frustrated and feeling burned out

Even if your work is deeply important to you, think about what it does if you fill every available hour with it.

For a relationship to last, it means spending time with each other. It means spending time with family and other people who are important to you.

 **ACTIVITY 7.3.2**

Identify ideas and take notes on how you can set boundaries and make time.

Tips to Make Time

There should be time that you all agree to spend together that is sacred – time that you schedule in, and you don't give up on.

☐ **Identify a time** that you will spend together. If it can be consistent, great, otherwise schedule this in each week

Define under which **specific circumstances** you might have to go help at work (this should be super rare, like massive crises only, if any)

☐ **Don't put work ahead of family.** If something comes up that will interrupt your family time, say **'No'**

☐ **Set limits** for how much you talk about work. Remember that there is more to life than what you do. There is more to your family's lives as well

☐ **Prioritize.** If you are spending all your time at work and your family is suffering, consider downscaling so that you can have more of a life without feeling pressure to always be working (if that's an issue)

☐ **Agree on what kind of details to share** about work and make time to talk in more detail if there is something really bothering you. Use the Sustainable Compartmenting skill for this

Even if you don't have a partner, thinking about these can help you prioritize time with family and friends, and help you get a better balance in life.

7.3.3 Active Constructive Responding

When someone shares something with you, they let you in on something meaningful in their lives. How you respond can either build a relationship or undermine it.

Broadly, the way you respond can be classified in two ways:

- **Active to Passive –** which is about how engaged you are in the conversation
- **Constructive to Destructive –** Which is about whether you enhance the moment or work against it

By combining these, we find four styles of responding. In the example below you can see this in action when someone tells you they got a new job:

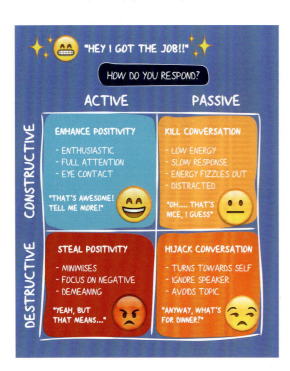

In the image you can see how three of the styles easily cut down the conversation and reverse the positivity of the moment. For example:

- **Passive constructive** means you are just too disinterested to respond. You might feel like you responded well, but instead you took the life out of the conversation
- **Passive destructive** is where you start talking about your own stuff instead and might not even bother talking about their news at all
- **Active destructive** is where you start focusing on the negatives of the news, minimizing it, and making demeaning comments

Each of these tends to harm a relationship, even if it's with a friend, family members or a child.

Active constructive responses (ACR) are the ones that build relationships. This is where you show that you truly care about their news. You're enthusiastic, you make eye contact, you drop other stuff you're doing, you ask follow-up questions (tell me more, how do you feel, etc), and overall show that you are excited for them.

The reason why you might tend toward the other styles is often due to exhaustion, being overworked and feeling lots of stress and pressure. These can put you in a gloomy mood and subconsciously make you want to withdraw or bring down the mood of others.

Being conscious of your response style and pushing yourself to use more ACR can do wonders for a relationship!

EXAMPLE

For a good example of ACR in action, watch this video - driv.ai/acr - or scan the code below:

SCAN ME

Strong Relationships in the Driven Resilience App

Scan the link to access the skill in the app (make sure you are **logged into the app** first).

app.hellodriven.com/activities/1241

ACTIVITY 7.3.3

Practice Active Constructive Responding. Tips:

- Show enthusiasm
- Make eye contact
- Be attentive
- Ask questions
- Show excitement

NOTES

COLLABORATION

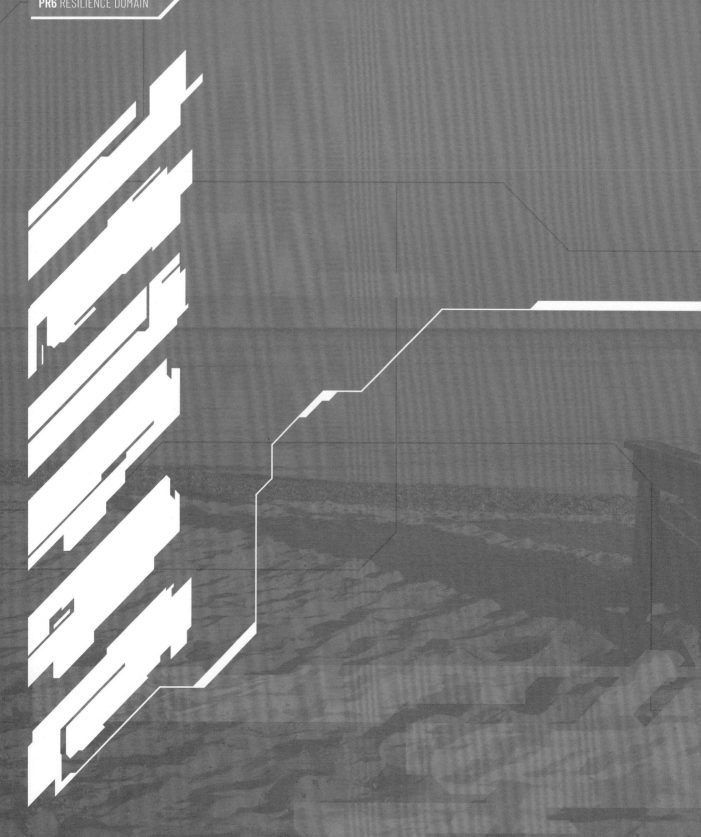

7.4

HIGH ADVERSITY
HUMOR

7.4 HIGH ADVERSITY HUMOR

Learing Outcomes:

- Learn about the benefits of using humor to help with high adversity work
- Learn about the four types of humor, and how to use humor at work
- Develop awareness of context and how to support humor

This is Useful For:

- Developing humor as a valuable technique to maintain motivation and manage the impact of difficult events

7.4.1 Humor – What & Why

Well, it's anything you find amusing. That's about as good an explanation as we're going to get without writing a book on the topic.

This means humor covers a very broad area, including everything from jokes through to really unexpected situations.

As Tibetan Buddhist monk Chogyam Trungpa said: *"A genuine sense of humor is having a light touch, not beating reality into the ground"*.

What about **High Adversity Humor (HAH)**?

HAH is generally about using humor as a **long-term strategy** to thrive in high adversity. This type of humor includes inside jokes where your co-workers and others in your field get it, but normally you wouldn't share that humor with 'outsiders'.

Humor is one of the most widely used coping techniques with emergency responders and others in high adversity jobs. Outsiders might often think *"How can you joke about something like that?"*

But when your job involves handling traumatic situations or crises daily then at some point you just have to laugh at the craziness of it all.

ONE OF THE **MOST** WIDELY-USED WAYS TO COPE.

SCAN ME

QUICK TEST

Humor at Work Check

Scan the code below to complete a short assessment about your experience of humor at work. You can do this assessment again later to see how your skill changes over time.

PS – make sure you are logged into your app to access this assessment.

app.hellodriven.com/activities/871

Why Use Humor

We often use humor without really thinking that much about why we use it. In high adversity occupations, humor helps to:

- Vent feelings
- Get social support
- Create distance

Let's explore these in more detail.

Vent Feelings

Often you will deal with really difficult situations. These can cause emotional reactions that are difficult to deal with and express. Humor is a way to vent those feelings in a way that doesn't feel so vulnerable.

For example, it might be hard to say *"That situation really affected me"*

While it may be a lot easier to say *"Well, that was f#####%$@d uuuuuup!"*

In a way it lets you be a lot more honest than you might otherwise be, helping to acknowledge how terrible something might have been and emotionally process it better.

Get Social Support

Following on from venting feelings, humor is often used in social settings where it helps you to form stronger connections with your co-workers and get social support. Being able to joke about the tough parts of the work is a useful way to connect and realize that, *"Yeah, we're all dealing with this stuff together!"*

Interestingly, you don't even necessarily have to be with someone – sometimes just imagining what someone else would think of a situation or a joke you thought of is enough to make you laugh about it.

Create Distance

When it's your job to deal with really difficult situations, feeling the full emotional impact of the situation each time can burn out anyone. Humor helps you to think about a situation in a less severe way, helping you get your job done. It doesn't make the situation any less terrible, but sometimes just the extremity of a situation can be something to laugh about.

Sometimes this is about finding amusement in incongruity, meaning things are very different from how you expect. Like when people find out that baby carrots are made from normal-size carrots. There might be an element of shock and horror, but it's also kind of funny.

Being able to maintain a sense of humor about traumatic situations can lead to some level of desensitization, which helps many to work in a detached yet empathic way. This helps to act professionally and more objectively, leading to more effective work without being negatively affected by the harshness of the situation.

NOTES

....
....
....
....
....
....
....
....
....
....
....

ACTIVITY 7.4.1

Where and how do you use humor so far in your work?

▲ ....

▲ ....

▲ ....

▲ ....

▲ ....

▲ ....

▲ ....

▲ ....

▲ ....

▲ ....

▲ ....

▲ ....

▲ ....

▲ ....

▲ ....

▲ ....

▲ ....

▲ ....

▲ ....

▲ ....

7.4.2 Your Body & Brain on Humor

We all tend to subconsciously understand the effect of humor – it makes us feel less stressed, more relaxed. After all, humor is fun! Though what does this look like in the brain itself?

◢ **Stress hormones like cortisol are reduced** leading to less nervousness and less anxiety

◢ The **limbic brain is calmed down** which makes you feel calmer and more focused

◢ The **prefrontal cortex gets more blood flow** helping you to think more clearly, be more resourceful, and get the job done more effectively

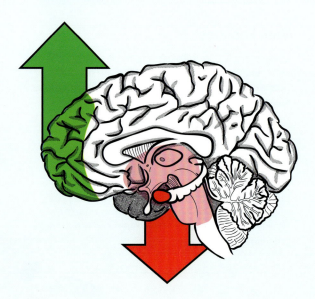

Within the brain humor also has an important role in terms of its connection with emotion and memories...

Emotion-Memory Connection

Experiences and memories are often connected with emotions. This means that when you refer to a memory, you tend to re-experience the emotion. For example, you remember something funny that happened yesterday and immediately start giggling at how ridiculous it was.

Though memories are funny like that, so to speak, since you can connect different emotions to them later.

- For example, let's say you had a difficult experience that was rough on you at the time, connecting an emotion of fear to it

- Later you tell a co-worker about the story, and as you go through the details, you both unexpectedly start laughing at how crazy the situation was

- The humor in that moment as you both laugh at it can then start to overpower the fear you felt back then

- When you remember the situation again, you might rather remember how you both laughed at it, re-experiencing the humor rather than the original fear

This example shows how the brain can remap emotional connections to memories, and how humor can even help to deal with old traumas.

What About Your Health?

Humor benefits your health too. In areas including:

- Less tense muscles
- Better breathing and respiratory functioning
- Improved blood circulation
- Increased pain-dulling endorphins

There are even connections to better heart health, so having a laugh is simply the responsible thing to do.

ACTIVITY 7.4.2

What effects have you noticed when you use humor?

....
....
....
....
....
....
....
....
....
....
....
....
....
....
....
....
....
....
....
....

ACTIVITY 7.4.3

What type of humor do you tend to use? What about your team?

Affiliative - Self-enhancing - Self-defeating - Aggressive

....
....
....
....
....
....
....
....
....
....
....
....
....
....
....
....
....
....
....
....

7.4.3 Types of Humor

Especially in the workplace, there are certain types of humor that are worth exploring:

- **Affiliative –** Using humor to build relationships through amusing others in a positive and self-accepting way
- **Self-enhancing –** Finding the silver lining in tough situations, or laughing at yourself or the situation to keep yourself motivated and positive
- **Self-defeating –** An attempt at gaining approval of others through making disparaging remarks about yourself
- **Aggressive –** Targeting other people to amuse yourself or others

Let's explore each of these further.

Affiliative Humor

This is a generally positive use of humor that doesn't target anyone. This mostly involves other people which helps you build relationships with people, making it one that's very appropriate in the workplace. Examples include:

- Making puns
- Witty remarks (that don't target anyone)
- Sharing jokes (*"I haven't slept for 10 days, because that would be too long."*)
- Funny pictures and videos

Provided you're not getting carried away and spending more time looking for something to joke about rather than getting work done, then this style is generally positive.

Self-Enhancing Humor

This style is one you can use by yourself or with others, and it mostly involves being able to **see the good or the funny side of any situation**, even when it's very difficult.

An example would be to find yourself in a horrifying situation and saying, *"I wouldn't want to be anywhere else!"*

Obviously, that's a joke and other people get it right away, but it lightens the mood at that moment, and sometimes you accidentally believe yourself and feel more motivated to get things done! It's funny how the words you use program your own beliefs.

In your line of work, this is a skill that is useful and important to use.

Self-Defeating Humor

Making jokes at your own expense can show others that you don't take yourself too seriously. This can be a useful way to build relationships with people.

For example, if you are very confident and a highly capable person, using self-defeating humor can be useful to remind people that you are but a mere mortal and you don't see yourself as better than them (even if you'd likely beat them in a contest of wit and skill).

Though, when humor has a target, it easily slips into negative territory - even if that target is yourself. Too much use of self-defeating humor can cause others to see you as seeking validation and pity.

Aggressive (Inappropriate) Humor

Aggressive humor generally targets someone in some way. While it might be funny for you or a few other people, it usually means someone is being harmed or disparaged in some way, meaning it's not appropriate in the workplace. Examples include:

- **Negative social comparison –** Making fun of someone by making yourself seem superior to them. Even making fun of people in other emergency response fields can be harmful and lead to destructive rivalries. There's a line between teasing and seeing yourself as better than someone else
- **Victim blaming –** Making fun of people because of the bad things that happened to them due to something they did (e.g. someone getting cancer from smoking)
- **Schadenfreude –** A German word for taking pleasure in others getting harmed (such as laughing at someone hit in the head by a ball thrown by a co-worker)
- **Pranks –** These involve embarrassing or harming someone else for the amusement of yourself and others. Things like 'prank wars' can lead people to live in fear of what will happen next. It might be intended in a 'good-natured' way, but it usually ends up being mean.

7.4.4 Context & Support

The reality of HAH is that it works inside your field. Meaning, it often doesn't translate well with others. For that reason, there needs to be an awareness of the context that you are in, since other people might think you're being insensitive.

These days, everyone with a phone can record what is being said, upload it to a social network and spark a frenzy of outrage about the incident. Even though this humor is an important method to cope with the stress you face, regular people might not get it and demand the people involved be fired. This can be tragic, but that's the reality of the world we live in now.

Because of this, try to make sure you're not being recorded, and be aware of the kind of slang and comments you might use when out in public.

Of course, there are many people out there that enjoy the same type of humor. This is often seen through tv shows that have a lot of dark humor, though that's not representative of everyone.

 **ACTIVITY 7.4.4**

How can you use or support humor more to help with your work?

Supporting Humor

If you're not a naturally funny person, then all isn't lost! Everyone in the workplace also has a role in supporting humor.

This means:

☐ **Be willing to laugh –** If something's funny, then show it! Some people feel they need to be super serious which can lead to others finding them hard to relate to. Simply allowing yourself to laugh is a simple and highly effective way to connect with people

☐ **Participate –** If the whole team is recording a Tik Tok video, then join in. You might just accidentally enjoy yourself (unless Tik Tok is banned for you, in which case make sure no one uses it...)

☐ **Call out aggressive humor –** Someone needs to set the tone as well in terms of what is out of order. If you see people using aggressive humor styles, call it out and push for more positive styles of humor

☐ **Lower your standards –** Yes that's right. Don't wait for super rare top shelf jokes before you allow yourself a sensible chuckle. Be willing to laugh at the silly stuff too. After all, people with expensive taste miss out on the simple pleasures

The idea is not for humor to get so carried away that no work gets done. But rather to use it to strengthen relationships, deal with tough situations and emotions, and ultimately help you and the whole team to be stronger together.

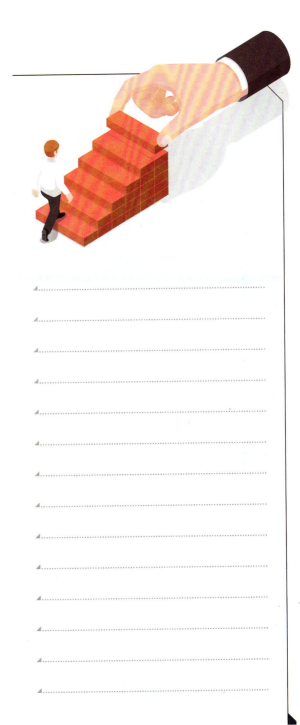

NOTES

....
....
....
....
....
....
....
....
....
....
....
....
....
....
....
....
....
....
....
....
....
....
....

High Adversity Humor in the Driven Resilience App

Scan the link to access the skill in the app (make sure you are **logged into the app** first).

app.hellodriven.com/activities/1242

NOTES

GLOSSARY

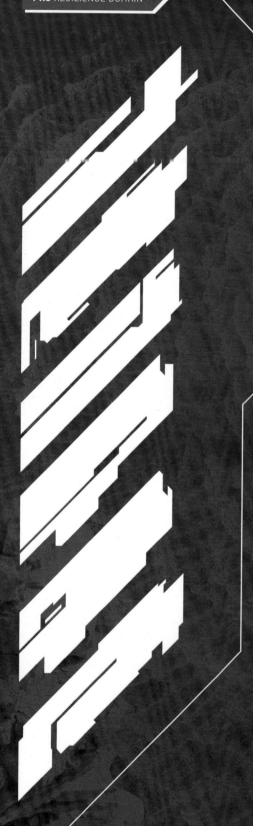

8.0

QR CODES, IMAGES, ACTIVITIES LIST

GLOSSARY

List of activities

PR6

VISION
- PURPOSE & MEANING
- PRIORITIES
- GOALS
- ALIGNMENT & CONGRUENCE

COMPOSURE
- STRESS MANAGEMENT
- EMOTIONAL AWARENESS
- CALM & IN CONTROL
- MINDFULNESS

COLLABORATION
- GOOD RELATIONSHIPS
- SOCIAL CONFIDENCE
- SUPPORT NETWORKS
- TRUST & TEAMWORK

REASONING
- INTROSPECTION
- RESOURCEFULNESS
- PREVENTION & PLANNING
- ADAPTATION

TENACITY
- PERSISTENCE
- MOTIVATION
- REALISTIC OPTIMISM
- BOUNCE BACK

HEALTH
- HEALTH VIEWS & GOALS
- NUTRITION HABITS
- SLEEP QUALITY
- EXERCISE HABITS

HART Risk Factors

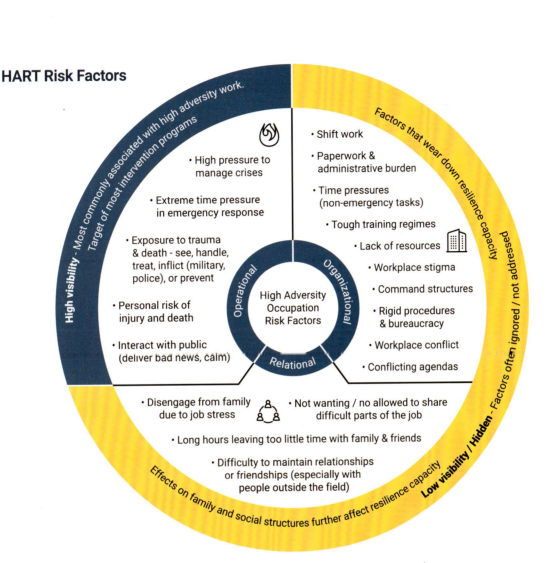

High visibility - Most commonly associated with high adversity work. Target of most intervention programs

Operational

- High pressure to manage crises
- Extreme time pressure in emergency response
- Exposure to trauma & death - see, handle, treat, inflict (military, police), or prevent
- Personal risk of injury and death
- Interact with public (deliver bad news, calm)

Factors that wear down resilience capacity

Organizational

- Shift work
- Paperwork & administrative burden
- Time pressures (non-emergency tasks)
- Tough training regimes
- Lack of resources
- Workplace stigma
- Command structures
- Rigid procedures & bureaucracy
- Workplace conflict
- Conflicting agendas

High Adversity Occupation Risk Factors

Low visibility / Hidden - Factors often ignored / not addressed

Relational

- Disengage from family due to job stress
- Not wanting / no allowed to share difficult parts of the job
- Long hours leaving too little time with family & friends
- Difficulty to maintain relationships or friendships (especially with people outside the field)

Effects on family and social structures further affect resilience capacity

Hart Program Approach

1. IDENTIFY STAKEHOLDERS

Leaders
Executive layer - key leaders and decision-makers required for top-level endorsement

Managers
All management and supervisory roles, through to managers of ground-level staff

Staff
Operational front-line workers, members, volunteers, and support staff

2. DESIGN SUSTAINABILITY

Culture Design
Clarify cultural goals to embed resilience as a key value of the organization. Agree on program elements needed to achieve cultural uplift and sustainability

Management Training
Educate management on risk factors and own responsibility to lead by example. Put meaningful effort into improving organizational risk factors

Coordinated Launch
Communicate to all staff through leaders and managers the program to be launched through coordinated campaign for high awareness

3. IMPLEMENT HART

Embed Champions
Ground-level and management staff to champion resilience

Workshops & Trainers
HART Instructors run certification workshops and live training

Assessments
PR6 assessment to track starting point and change over time

Digital Access (app)
Virtual delivery of training to scale ongoing reinforcement

Family Access
App and training webinars for family of staff to extend impact

4. EVALUATE & IMPROVE

Measure & Report
Ongoing assessment of progress across risk factors:
- Operational
- Organisational
- Relational

PR6 assessment to measure changes in resilience domains:
- Vision
- Composure,
- Reasoning
- Tenacity
- Collaboration
- Health

Track program impact and identify opportunities for improvement.

Improvement Loop Continually learn, enhance integration of program implementation. On-board new staff.

Mood Chart

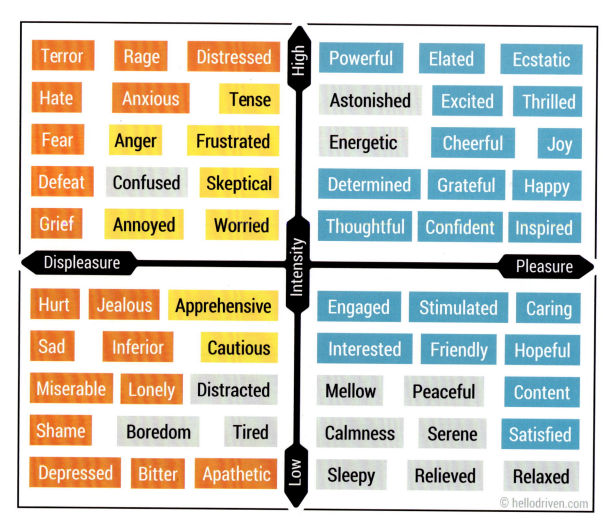

Legend

Constructive emotions   Neutral emotions

Constructive displeasure   Disruptive emotions

Are your emotions leading to useful and constructive actions?

Instant Techniques

These activities take you through the skills in this course in a step-by-step approach, making it easy to put them into practice in difficult moments. Make sure you are logged into the app and have a valid subscription to be able to access these. You can download the app with this code:

Get the
Driven Resilience App

1. Three Good Things
https://app.hellodriven.com/activities/791

2. Catch & Pause
https://app.hellodriven.com/activities/1024

3. Concrete Processing
https://app.hellodriven.com/activities/1023

4. Talk Through Grief
https://app.hellodriven.com/activities/864

5. Reappraisal
https://app.hellodriven.com/activities/152

6. Label Emotions
https://app.hellodriven.com/activities/150

7. Breathing Technique
https://app.hellodriven.com/activities/142

8. Overcoming a Mistake
https://app.hellodriven.com/activities/320

9. Incident Self-Debrief
https://app.hellodriven.com/activities/845

10. Sleep Meditation
https://app.hellodriven.com/activities/510

11. 14 Day Rewire Program
https://app.hellodriven.com/activities/511

HART Skills

Find these skills in the Driven Resilience App to learn more through an interactive approach. Check that you are logged into the app, and have a valid subscription to be able to access these.

1. Neuroscience
https://app.hellodriven.com/activities/1229

2. Connecting Purpose
https://app.hellodriven.com/activities/1230

3. Managing Work Hours
https://app.hellodriven.com/activities/1231

4. Compartmenting
https://app.hellodriven.com/activities/1232

5. Thoughts & Behaviors
https://app.hellodriven.com/activities/1233

6. Concrete Processing
https://app.hellodriven.com/activities/1234

7. Brain-Balanced Breathing
https://app.hellodriven.com/activities/1235

8. High Adversity Reappraisal
https://app.hellodriven.com/activities/1236

9. Mental Load Management
https://app.hellodriven.com/activities/1237

10. Three Good Things
https://app.hellodriven.com/activities/1238

11. High Quality Connections
https://app.hellodriven.com/activities/1239

12. Grief & Growth
https://app.hellodriven.com/activities/1240

13. Strong Relationships
https://app.hellodriven.com/activities/1241

14. High Adversity Humor
https://app.hellodriven.com/activities/1242

15. PR6 Resilience Skills
https://app.hellodriven.com/activities/449

Quick Tests

Check up on your progress with the assessments in the Driven Resilience App. Check that you are logged into the app, and have a valid subscription to be able to access these.

1. Compartmenting Skill
https://app.hellodriven.com/activities/780

2. Job Satisfaction
https://app.hellodriven.com/activities/799

3. Concrete Processing Skill
https://app.hellodriven.com/activities/793

4. Work Hours
https://app.hellodriven.com/activities/875

5. Engagement
https://app.hellodriven.com/activities/852

6. Carer Satisfaction
https://app.hellodriven.com/activities/873

7. Vicarious Exposure
https://app.hellodriven.com/activities/1227

8. Co-worker Connections
https://app.hellodriven.com/activities/854

9. Humor at Work
https://app.hellodriven.com/activities/871

10. Work Context
https://app.hellodriven.com/activities/957

RESEARCH

The **High Adversity Resilience Training** program and the **Predictive 6 Factor Resilience Model** both are supported by extensive research. Hello Driven, developers of these programs, have published original research papers expanding on the historical evidence and neuroscience that enable the model and strategies to work effectively.

These original research papers, along with supporting references, can be found here as open access papers through the link or code below:

driv.ai/research